SpringerBriefs in Economics

For further volumes:
http://www.springer.com/series/8876

Abu S. Shonchoy
Editor

Seasonality and Microcredit

The Case of Northern Bangladesh

Springer

Editor
Abu S. Shonchoy
Institute of Developing Economies
Japan External Trade Organization
Chiba
Japan

ISSN 2191-5504 ISSN 2191-5512 (electronic)
ISBN 978-4-431-55009-9 ISBN 978-4-431-55010-5 (eBook)
DOI 10.1007/978-4-431-55010-5
Springer Tokyo Heidelberg New York Dordrecht London

Library of Congress Control Number: 2014940521

Printed on acid-free paper

Springer is part of Springer Science+Business Media (www.springer.com)

To my parents and my family,
Liza and Zunairah

Foreword

Seasonality and its impacts can be widespread for rural people dependent on agriculture in developing countries. Microfinance, which has been substantially contributing to poverty reduction in the context of Bangladesh, has great potential in reducing seasonal deprivation arising from agricultural cycles, which is characterized by lack of income opportunities, low wages, and high food prices. However, prototype microfinance requiring weekly repayments and regular meeting attendance do not appear to be consistent with the situation people face during the seasonality in northern Bangladesh as they are often forced to migrate elsewhere due to flooding and other calamities. This apparent paradox between prototype microfinance rules and living conditions in northwest Bangladesh is the point of departure of this book. This study investigates the effects of a seasonality-adjusted microcredit scheme (flexible repayment schedule) compared with those of a traditional scheme (inflexible repayment schedule) on food consumption during the period of seasonality in the context of Bangladesh. Prior empirical studies were motivated by a desire to identify the effect of microcredit on food consumption and other welfare indicators, and the focus of this study is to disentangle the effect of flexibility (of the repayment schedule) on certain welfare indicators, which is an important step forward to fill an important knowledge gap.

The study has several strengths, including the experimental design and the fact that it has favorable policy implications. The study has been carefully and competently executed and the results obtained are very important. The study, quite appropriately, applies randomized control trial (RCT) strategy to investigate the effect of a flexible microcredit scheme by varying the degree of flexibility between several treatments and a control group of microcredit recipients. RCT is regarded as the most powerful research design in drawing conclusions about the impact of any intervention on a specific outcome. Such a randomized experiment facilitates our understanding of whether any public program actually work in reaching their goals as well as the beneficiaries.

The findings reported in this book suggest that there is no impact of the flexibility on the short-term positive impact on food consumption. The results importantly suggest that on average microcredit ensures more secure food consumption for all borrowers regardless of flexibility. The results also suggest that flexible product design appears good on the part of providers, implying that the flexible payment schedule does not affect loan collection discipline contrary to the general belief of microfinance institutions. This is an important finding. The authors provide interesting and insightful explanations of the findings.

Overall this book addresses very important questions for designing microcredit schemes being offered for ultra-poor populations in developing countries and will serve as an important reference for researchers as well as policy makers. I am sure this book will be a valuable addition for researchers working in the field of microfinance and development issues and will define the scope for further research on next-generation microfinance schemes aiming at addressing food security and poverty reduction.

Dhaka, Bangladesh, January 2014

Dr. Minhaj Mahmud
Head of Research,
Institute of Governance Studies (IGS)
and BRAC Development Institute (BDI),
BRAC University,
Dhaka, Bangladesh

Preface

The mismatch between credit repayments and income seasonality can create serious distortions. However, typically Micro-Finance Institutes (MFIs) do not provide any adjustments due to the income seasonality. For instance in northern Bangladesh, income and consumption downfalls during the time of post-*Aman* rice plantation seasons are quite regular phenomenon which is locally known as *Monga*. Poor landless agricultural wage laborers suffer the most due to this seasonality and usually they face difficulty to smooth their consumptions. As a result, it is extremely difficult to arrange the regular weekly loan repayments of the microcredit, which they have taken during the productive part of the year. Using field experiments through RCTs in northern Bangladesh, we randomly assigned seasonality adjusted flexible microcredits and traditional rigid microcredit to different borrowing groups. Examining the repayment behavior of the borrowers in the context of geographical classifications and loan designs, employing both survey and experimental methods, this study allows us to see the consequences of flexible loan repayment rules during the lean periods, and how they affect both MFIs and participating borrowers. The findings of this study have important policy implications for MFIs and policy makers of the developing countries.

Acknowledgments

This study has been generously funded by the IDE Research Grant under the scheme of "New Strategies of Nations and Firms for Sustainable Development," 2011–2012. The authors would also like to acknowledge the support provided by the JSPS Grant-in-Aid for Scientific Research-S (22223003) under the project of "Poverty Reduction, Institutions, Markets, and Policies in Developing Countries: Toward a Theory of Comparative Economic Development" (PRIMCED), Hitotsubashi University. Ed Lucio of University of Tokyo and, Mohammad Helal Uddin and Nayamat Ullah Tasnim of University of Dhaka have given excellent research assistantship during the course of this study. The authors would also like to extend their thanks to four anonymous referees, who have given many valuable comments to improve this version of the chapters. Last but not least, special thanks to all the staff members of our counterpart NGO, Gana Unnayan Kendra (GUK) for their relentless efforts to make this study a success.

About the Editor

Dr. Abu S. Shonchoy is working as a research fellow at the Institute of Developing Economies (IDE) JETRO, Japan, and as an adjunct assistant professor at the Graduate School of Public Policy (GraSPP) at The University of Tokyo. He also holds a visiting fellowship position at the South Asian Network of Economic Modeling (SANEM). Prior to joining IDE-JETRO, he worked for BRAC University in Bangladesh and in ANU, UNSW, and UTS in Australia as a lecturer. He also worked for the International Monetary Fund (IMF), in Washington DC, USA, during the period of 2007–2008. Dr. Shonchoy is a development economist with interests in impact evaluation and microeconometrics. He has several ongoing field research projects in Bangladesh and in India. His current research interests include projects on microfinance, migration, electrification, and education. Dr. Shonchoy graduated from the University of Dhaka, Bangladesh, with a B.Sc. (Honors) in economics, a master's degree in economic policy from the Australian National University (ANU), and a Ph.D. in economics from the University of New South Wales (UNSW), Australia.

Contributors

Takashi Kurosaki Hitotsubashi University, Kunitachi, Tokyo, Japan

Abu S. Shonchoy Institute of Developing Economies, Japan External Trade Organization (IDE-JETRO), Mihama-ku, Chiba, Japan

Kazunari Tsukada Institute of Developing Economies, Japan External Trade Organization (IDE-JETRO), Mihama-ku, Chiba, Japan

Tatsufumi Yamagata Institute of Developing Economies, Japan External Trade Organization (IDE-JETRO), Mihama-ku, Chiba, Japan

Contents

Chapter 1
Introduction

Abu S. Shonchoy

Abstract This study aims to elucidate the mismatch between seasonality and the terms of microcredit, and to understand the impact of seasonality-adjusted microcredit. To do this, an RCT based experiment has been employed to evaluate the general claims of NGOs regarding moratoria during times of seasonality-induced hardship. Making use of both survey and experimental methods, the findings of this study will allow us to understand the consequences of flexible loan repayment rules during the lean periods, and how they affect both MFIs and participating borrowers.

Keywords Microcredit · Randomized controlled trial · Seasonality · Northern Bangladesh

Neither the term "seasonality" nor its impact on agrarian societies is uncommon in the developing world.[1] Seasonality, which is often spoken of in terms of "lean periods," can occur due to agricultural cycles or natural disasters, such as droughts, flooding, cyclones, climate change, or river erosion. Given the current global move to fight poverty and hunger, it is very important to understand the seasonal dimension of the poverty and hunger nexus, which affects the poor of developing countries regularly and repeatedly. Agriculture-dependent rural poverty—which is mostly prevalent in Southeast Asia and Sub-Saharan Africa—can be linked to such distinct crop-cycle-based seasonality. Such a phenomenon becomes more severe when coupled with adverse seasonal climatic conditions that can lead to poor-quality harvests or outright crop failure (Chambers et al. 1981). Moreover, inadequate access to formal credit and insurance products further traps people in chronic and inter-generational poverty—poverty that is very difficult to tackle through the use of general public policy measures and social safety net approaches.

[1] See, for example, Destombes (2006) and Ludden (1999).

A. S. Shonchoy (✉)
Institute of Developing Economies, Japan External Trade Organization,
3-2-2 Wakaba, Mihama-ku, Chiba-shi 261-8545, Japan
e-mail: parves.shonchoy@gmail.com

A. S. Shonchoy (ed.), *Seasonality and Microcredit*, SpringerBriefs in Economics,
DOI: 10.1007/978-4-431-55010-5_1,

For example, in Bangladesh, the term "seasonality" is associated with a seasonal food deprivation phenomenon known locally as *monga*; it is most common in northern Bangladesh (Khandker and Mahmud 2012). Rural life in Bangladesh very much revolves around the agricultural cycle, which is characterized by three crop seasons that are in turn based on three categories of rice: Aus (December/January–March), Boro (March/April–June/July), and *Aman* (July/August–November/December). As a consequence of this cycle, two major seasonal deficits occur: one from late September to early November, and the other from late March to early May. With the widespread expansion of Boro cultivation, the incidence of the early summer lean period has significantly declined. However, the autumn lean season that follows the plantation of the *Aman* crop still affects most parts of the country, especially the northern part of Bangladesh (Khandker and Mahmud 2012). Almost no alternative agricultural activity takes place in that period, and the non-agricultural sector cannot sufficiently absorb the seasonally unemployed labor.

During the lean season, drastic drops in employment-led income constitute the major reason behind reduced food consumption; this has been well documented in the literature (e.g., Rahman 1995). During the lean season, such a lack of income and alternative means for obtaining earnings limit the purchasing power of the people, and this situation cannot be mitigated with the minuscule amounts of assets and savings that poor households typically carry. Anecdotal evidence suggests that the average number of meals consumed is significantly reduced during *monga*, and families with young and elderly members suffer the most. The absence of a functional credit market stops households from smoothing their consumption (Pitt and Khandker 2002). As a result, many individuals borrow from landlords or informal money lenders—both of which tend to charge very high interest rates—and they subsequently fall into a debt trap.

Given this situation, various coping strategies have emerged among the *monga*-affected people of northern Bangladesh. Other than borrowing from informal sources that charge high interest rates, coping strategies common among the *monga*-affected people include the advance sale of labor (Khandker and Mahmud 2012), the purchase of household essentials on credit, skipping meals during the lean season (Berg and Emran 2011), and seasonal migration (Shonchoy 2011). Of these coping strategies, temporary seasonal migration to urban areas appears to be a relatively practical and rational strategy, as individuals can move from rural areas to nearby urban areas or cities for a short period of time in an attempt to earn a livelihood during this lean season. However, such a migration strategy is not suitable for everyone because of family constraints (especially among households with female heads or disabled heads that may not be able to migrate during the lean season). In addition, credit and financing constraints, a lack of networking, and asymmetric information problems limit an individual's ability to migrate (Bryan et al. 2012).

One recent policy development in developing countries has been the emergence of microcredit institutions that focus on poverty alleviation. It is argued that, given access to even small amounts of credit, entrepreneurs from poor households will find opportunities to engage in viable income-generating activities (IGA)—many of which will be secondary to their primary occupations—and thus ameliorate poverty on their own. Microcredit is accessible in rural areas through microfinance institutions (MFIs), which have proliferated quite rapidly in recent years. According to the Microcredit Summit Campaign, as of 2011, there were 195 million microcredit borrowers,[2] of whom more than 100 million were women. In 2006, Mohammad Yunus and the Grameen Bank were awarded the Nobel Prize for Peace for their contributions to poverty reduction, especially in Bangladesh. However, among academics, there is thus far no consensus on the impact of microcredit on income improvement and poverty reduction (Banerjee et al. 2009). On the one hand, various studies on the impact of microcredit in developing countries have found evidence of consumption-smoothing, asset-building (Pitt and Khandker 1998), and poverty reduction (Khandker 2005). Conversely, using the same dataset as that used by Pitt and Khandker (1998), Morduch (1999) found that the average impact of microfinance is "nonexistent." Similarly, Navajas et al. (2000) conclude that microcredit is largely unsuccessful in reaching the poor and the vulnerable.

A major drawback of the microcredit framework is its rigid loan repayment system (Karlan and Mullainathan 2007). Nearly all loan contracts are fixed in their repayment schedules, which involve consistent and equal weekly payments along with a high interest rate. However, MFIs work with poor rural people who most often have uncertain and infrequent incomes, and these circumstances make it very difficult for them to maintain such rigid weekly loan repayments. Especially during the lean period—when there are no jobs available in the rural agricultural sector—it can be very difficult for the poor to generate income, let alone comply with a loan repayment scheme. Indeed, to say that rigid weekly repayments during the time of seasonal hardship exacerbate their misery is an understatement. It was found that during *monga* households take extreme measures, like selling productive assets (Khandker and Mahmud 2012) or borrowing from loan sharks who charge extraordinarily high interest rates, to maintain a clean record of repayment of microcredit and be assured of access to future microcredit loans from the MFIs.

Using primary data from rural households in Bangladesh, Shonchoy (2009a, b) shows that during the lean season, access to microcredit does not increase the income levels of individuals, compared to those with no access to credit, *ceteris paribus*. Additionally, Shonchoy (2009a, b) at the time of the survey found no MFI that operates any well-targeted microfinance program that is solely dedicated to tackling seasonality issues such as *monga*. Given that seasonality in northern Bangladesh is historically well known, it is particularly puzzling to find that no leading microcredit product—save for the PRIME intervention by PKSF—has been designed to mitigate the effects of seasonality by providing some form of moratorium on loan repayments during *monga*.[3]

---

[2] http://www.microcreditsummit.org

[3] PRIME (Programmed Initiatives for Monga Eradication) was introduced in 2006 by PKSF (Palli Karma–Sahayak Foundation), a microcredit wholesaler and umbrella organization in Bangladesh. Under the PRIME scheme, individual nongovernment organizations (NGOs) receive credit facilities that have "flexible" terms, under which these NGOs are free to negotiate the

The mismatch between credit repayments and income can create serious distortions that for some people deepen the debt trap, especially if they take extreme measures to repay their loans on a weekly basis during the lean period. In this study, we examine whether these distortions are inevitable. If MFIs could allow some flexibility in the microcredit repayment schedules—especially in periods of uncertain income during lean periods, or following natural disasters—this may improve the livelihoods of the poor, provide them with greater flexibility and mobility, and, in turn, improve their capacity to repay their loans. Currently, MFIs are reluctant to relax their loan repayment rules. It seems that they fear that allowing people a moratorium on a weekly repayment scheme during the lean period may adversely affect their debt repayment discipline; possibly the fear is that borrowers could become behaviorally accustomed to making lower or no repayments when those payments are nonetheless required, and that this might ultimately lead to lower recovery rates or even higher default rates.

Given this trade-off, it appears that an appropriate way to address these issues is the introduction of a field experiment that features a randomized controlled trial (RCT). The RCT is the new "gold standard" for empirical research, as it clearly identifies causality issues and evaluates impacts.[4] Strong in terms of empirical validity, the RCT is now being implemented by many applied researchers to evaluate many puzzling and unsolved issues that relate to development questions and impact evaluations. Interestingly, a large number of RCT studies have been undertaken in microfinance-related research, which covers a wide range of subjects, including the impact of microfinance (Banerjee et al. 2009), weekly versus monthly repayments (Field and Pande 2008), group versus individual liability (Giné and Karlan 2009), random variations in meeting frequency (Feigenberg et al. 2011), and variance in a loan's term structure (Field and Pande 2011), to name just a few. However, to the best of our knowledge, no study thus far has addressed the customization of microcredit repayment schedules that adjust for local seasonality. As such, this will be a pioneering study in the field of seasonality-adjusted flexible microcredit that is both geographically and seasonally adjusted to help the vulnerable and lean season-affected poor cope better with periods of hardship.

The aim of this study is to elucidate the mismatch between seasonality and the terms of microcredit, and to understand the impact of seasonality-adjusted microcredit. To do this, it uses an RCT to evaluate the general claims of NGOs regarding moratoria during times of seasonality-induced hardship. Making use of both survey and experimental methods, the findings of this study will allow us to

---

(Footnote 3 continued)
credit amount, repayment schedule, and frequency of meetings with the beneficiary, and impose completely different sets of schemes with various borrowing groups. While this is to some extent ideal for the beneficiaries, it is not easy to evaluate flexibility in terms that improve the accessibility of beneficiaries to microfinance, the performance in IGA, or the livelihoods of their families.

[4] Nonetheless, RCT studies are not always free from endogeneity bias, as has been shown in a recent study by Barrett and Carter (2010).

understand the consequences of flexible loan repayment rules during the lean periods, and how they affect both MFIs and participating borrowers.

Microcredit schemes have improved rural residents' access to the formal credit market. However, we need to understand the possible loopholes and side effects of such instruments, and find ways to improve them. The results of this study will be of importance to both poor borrowers, and the MFIs and policy-makers who support them. If we find that a relaxation of repayment schemes gives rise to improved welfare without inducing higher risk among MFIs, these institutions will be more likely to revise their contracts to the benefit of the poor. If we find that the associated risk is too high, then either policy-makers can compensate MFIs in bearing those risks or we can look for other ways to alleviate the problem. For example, government and donor agencies may want to focus more on capacity-building among the populace in terms of nurturing a diversity of alternative skills among both agricultural and non-agricultural professionals—skills that would help them establish a more viable livelihood strategy during the lean season. Alternatively, policy-makers could design their own targeted safety net for seasonality-affected people.

The analysis depicted in this book was undertaken through the use of survey data collected both before and after the RCT intervention. In our RCT design, we first formed typical microfinance groups from 72 randomly chosen villages in the Gaibandha and Kurigram districts of Bangladesh. Our NGO counterpart, Gana Unnayan Kendra (GUK), used its own household selection criteria to choose groups, each of which contained 20 members. Borrowers obtained a line of credit of BDT 3,000 and began to make repayments after a short, two-week grace period. The repayments were made in 45 installments, each of which amounted to BDT 75, implying a gross interest payment of BDT 360 spread across the borrowing period of approximately one year. Each of the weekly installments was to be repaid at a weekly meeting by the borrower. (The borrower was obliged to attend weekly meetings, even during the *monga* period.) We consider this scheme a traditional or inflexible microcredit scheme, and denote it as the "Control."

To understand the impact of repayment flexibility, as discussed, for the treatment group, the repayment schedule was relaxed in two ways during *monga*. The specific period designated as *monga* in the treatment is September 20–December 20. Under the first treatment, "Flexible 1," the borrower was temporarily given a moratorium during the designated *monga* period, during which households within the Flexible 1 groups did not pay any installments. After the *monga* period was over, these borrowers began to pay BDT 100 per week so that their total repayment amount and repayment period were identical to those of the Control group.

As a variation of the first treatment, one-third of those treated with Flexible 1 were also given IGA support; we refer to this treatment as "Flexible 1 + IGA." Under IGA support, instead of being given cash, microcredit borrowers received a productive asset of their choice within the credit amount. They were also given advice in utilizing that asset, but no further subsidy was provided.

Under the second flexibility treatment, during the designated *monga* period, the repayment scheme changed so as to demand three monthly installments of BDT

300 each. After the *monga* period, borrowers resumed paying BDT 75 per week so that their total repayment amount and repayment period were identical to those of the Control group. We refer to this treatment as "Flexible 2."

In all, we randomly selected 12 villages for "Control," 24 for "Flexible 1," 12 for "Flexible 1 + IGA," and 24 for "Flexible 2." In each village, a borrower group known as *Samity* was formed, comprising 20 members. Of these, 15 members were randomly selected in September 2011 to receive a line of microcredit of BDT 3,000. The remaining five members did not receive microcredit in 2011, but remained in the group as observers. We surveyed these 1,440 households both before (baseline) and after one year of intervention (endline). We also executed a short *monga* survey during the *monga* of 2011 in order to understand the severity of the seasonal conditions faced by the people of northern Bangladesh. The empirical analysis outlined in this book was undertaken using these baseline data from 2011, endline data from 2012, and information from a short *monga* survey in 2011.

This book is organized as follows. Chapter 2 talks about the overall microfinance scenario. It reviews selected literature on the rigidity and flexibility of microcredit contracts and also provides a quick overview of the microfinance revolution and its current presence in various parts of the world. Chapter 3 deals with the seasonality-affected region of northern Bangladesh and the overall microcredit scenario of Bangladesh. Chapter 4 analyzes the socioeconomic circumstances of the sampled areas by examining survey data. Chapter 5 draws attention to the core component of this research by discussing the timeline of the survey and the details of the experiment, including its design. Chapter 6 provides a detailed analysis of the repayment behavior of the borrowers. Chapter 7 focuses on the impact study of flexible microcredit on food consumption during the lean period, and Chap. 8 provides concluding remarks.

References

Banerjee A, Duflo E, Glennerster R, Kinnan C (2009). The miracle of microfinance? Evidence from a randomized evaluation. J-PAL working paper

Barrett CB, Carter MR (2010) The power and pitfalls of experiments in development economics: some non-random reflections. Appl Econ Perspect Policy 32(4):515–548

Berg C, Emran MS (2011) Does Microfinance Help the ultrapoor cope with seasonal shocks? Evidence from seasonal famine (Monga) in Bangladesh. SSRN eLibrary

Bryan G, Chowdhury S, Mobarak A (2012) Seasonal migration and risk aversion. CEPR discussion paper no. DP8739. Available at SSRN: http://ssrn.com/abstract=1988671

Chambers R, Longhurst R, Pacey A (1981) Seasonal dimensions to rural poverty. Frances Pinter, London

Destombes J (2006) From long-term patterns of seasonal hunger to changing experiences of everyday poverty: Northeastern Ghana c. 1930–2000. J Afr Hist 47(2):181–205

Feigenberg B, Field E, Pande R (2011) The economic returns to social interaction: experimental evidence from microfinance. Harvard University, Cambridge

Field E, Pande R (2008) Repayment frequency and default in microfinance: evidence from india. J Eur Econ Assoc 6(2–3):501–509

Field E, Pande R (2011) Term structure of debt and entrepreneurship: experimental evidence from microfinance. Harvard University working paper

Giné X, Karlan D (2009). Group versus individual liability: long-term evidence from Philippine microcredit lending groups. Economic Growth Center, Yale University, New Haven, CT, USA

Karlan D, Mullainathan S (2007) Is microfinance too rigid? VoxEU. Dec 2007

Khandker SR, Mahmud W (2012) Seasonal hunger and public policies: evidence from Northwest Bangladesh. World Bank Publications, Washington DC

Khandker SR (2005) Microfinance and poverty: evidence using panel data from Bangladesh. World Bank Econ Rev 19(2):263–286

Ludden D (1999) Agrarian history of South Asia. Cambridge University Press, Cambridge

Morduch J (1999) The Microfinance Promise. J Econo Lit 37(4):1569–1614

Navajas S, Schreiner M, Meyer RL, Gonzalez-Vega C, Rodriguez-Meza J (2000) Microcredit and the poorest of the poor: theory and evidence from Bolivia. World Dev 28(2):333–346

Pitt MA, Khandker SA (1998) The impact of group-based credit programs on poor households in Bangladesh: does the gender of participants matter? J Polit Econ 106(5):958–996

Pitt MM, Khandker SR (2002) Credit programmes for the poor and seasonality in rural Bangladesh. J Dev Stud 39(2):1–24

Rahman HZ (1995) Mora Kartik: seasonal deficits and the vulnerability of the rural poor. In: Rahman HZ, Hossain M (eds) Rethinking rural poverty: Bangladesh as a case study. Sage Publications, New Dehli

Shonchoy A (2009a) Seasonal migration and micro-credit in the lean period: evidence from Bangladesh. Presented on the conference Bangladesh on 21st century at Harvard University

Shonchoy A (2009b) Essays in development economics, unpublished Ph.D dissertation, University of New South Wales, Kensington

Shonchoy AS (2011) Seasonal migration and micro-credit in the lean period: evidence from Northwest Bangladesh. IDE discussion paper no. 294, Japan

Chapter 2
Microcredit Revisited: Towards More Flexible Loan Contracts

Kazunari Tsukada

Abstract Group liability and a fixed repayment schedule with frequent installments are prominent features of microcredit loan contracts. These rules make it possible for lenders to reduce lending costs and provide borrowers with appropriate incentives to repay. Sometimes they facilitate mutual insurance among members and improve the welfare of borrowers by providing a commitment device that induces saving-like behaviors. However, they also impose considerable burdens on borrowers. This chapter reviews selected literature on the rigidity and flexibility of microcredit contracts and provides an overview of the microfinance revolution and its current presence in various parts of the world.

Keywords Group liability · Repayment mechanism · Commitment device · Microcredit

2.1 Introduction

Many economists believe that the absence of well-functioning credit markets has been one of the major obstacles to the alleviation of global poverty. Expanding credit access can help those who receive credit allocate resources efficiently over time and effectively cope with risk; in this way, credit access can improve economic opportunities for the poor. However, despite the apparent benefits, the poor often find it difficult to obtain credit. In a traditional loan contract, a lender usually requires collateral to secure the loan, should the borrower be unable to make the loan repayments. However, the poor rarely have sufficient assets for use as collateral. In the absence of collateral, the lender incurs all the loss associated with

K. Tsukada (✉)
Institute of Developing Economies, Japan External Trade Organization (IDE-JETRO), 3-2-2 Wakaba, Mihama-ku, Chiba 261-8545, Japan
e-mail: Kazunari_Tsukada@ide.go.jp

A. S. Shonchoy (ed.), *Seasonality and Microcredit*, SpringerBriefs in Economics,
DOI: 10.1007/978-4-431-55010-5_2,

a loan default. To mitigate the risk of repayment failure, therefore, substantial efforts need to be made in screening, monitoring, and enforcing loan terms. In general, these efforts are too costly for the uninformed lender to be adequately compensated by interest revenue from the very small loans that the poor typically need.

In the last several decades, microcredit institutions have introduced a series of small and uncollateralized loan products for the poor. Microcredit now flourishes worldwide. In discussing the remarkable success of microcredit—which was widely acknowledged when Muhammad Yunus and the Grameen Bank were awarded the 2006 Nobel Peace Prize—a number of possible mechanisms have been suggested by which microcredit could address the problems that traditional lending programs face. Although the debate is ongoing, two notable features of microcredit—namely, group liability lending and a fixed repayment schedule with frequent installments—have attracted considerable attention (Armendariz and Morduch 2010). Both features are thought to be important mechanisms through which a lender could maintain high repayment rates. However, it is also necessary to note that these two features impose considerable costs on borrowers. Under group liability lending, any costs associated with the failure to repay must be incurred by the group borrowers, and this may create tension among them. Frequent repayments also increase the direct costs of attending the meetings where repayments take place either weekly, bi-weekly, or monthly. Furthermore, a fixed schedule eliminates any possibility of a borrower being able to adjust the amount of an installment in line with his or her economic conditions; the borrower must repay a fixed amount, even in times of hardship. Being aware of the costs related to rigidity, MFIs are currently trying to convert their portfolios into more flexible loan products. A central problem now is how to balance flexibility and repayment discipline without incurring a higher rate of defaults.

In this chapter, we review selected literature on the rigidity and flexibility of microcredit contracts. We focus, in particular, on issues regarding group liability and repayment rules, as they supposedly play significant roles in making microfinance contracts more successful and, at the same time, more rigid. It is important to examine the potential benefits of more flexible loan contracts. By offering financial services that are tailored to client demands, flexible loan contracts may increase the total number of beneficiaries and improve client welfare. According to previous studies, microcredit goals have not yet been achieved in terms of outreach and overall impact (Armendariz and Morduch 2010; Kono and Takahashi 2010).

This chapter is organized as follows. Section 2.2 discusses the costs and benefits of group liability lending. It also reviews the recent literature comparing group and individual liability lending. Section 2.3 examines the role of a fixed repayment schedule that features frequent installments. Based on the literature, we show that repayment frequency has its merits in offering a commitment device for the poor. Nonetheless, some costs dovetail from rigidity, especially when a client's income fluctuates over time. The final section provides concluding remarks.

2.2 From Group to Individual Liability Lending

2.2.1 Economics of Group Liability Lending

Many early studies on microfinance focused on the economics of group liability. Under group liability lending, members of a voluntarily formed group are jointly liable, either implicitly or explicitly, for one another's repayments. When one borrower cannot repay his or her loan, the other group members are required to repay on his or her behalf. All the group members are denied future loans until the entire group loan has been repaid in full. This innovative style of lending was pioneered by the Grameen Bank in Bangladesh (the classic Grameen model) and has subsequently been employed by many imitators worldwide. Group liability was so prominent in initial microfinance activities that it was considered a distinguishing aspect of contract design that worked in successful lending to the poor while establishing high repayment rates. To date, a number of theoretical models have identified various mechanisms—including peer screening (Ghatak 1999), peer monitoring (Stiglitz 1990; Varian 1990), and peer enforcement (Besley and Coate 1995)—through which group liability enables a lender to make uncollateralized loans to the poor. Ghatak and Guinnane (1999) provide a review of the early theoretical literature. A basic and rather simple idea that is found within theoretical approaches is shared by almost all existing models: shifting the burden of default from a lender to a group provides borrowers with appropriate incentives to use their local information and social ties, and to ensure repayments by peers within the same group.

One such mechanism, peer screening, works at the group formation stage. When a group is formed, potential borrowers wish to be paired with safe borrowers; this is because risky borrowers have a high probability of default, and the burden of their missed payments must be borne by the other group members. Hence, group liability effectively increases the interest rate for borrowers who are paired with risky partners. If agents know each other's level of reliability, risky borrowers will be avoided by safe borrowers and assortative matching will emerge as an equilibrium structure. Peer screening can thus differentiate effective interest rates between safe and risky groups. Lower effective interest rates can be imposed on safe groups, while risky groups face higher effective interest rates. This implicit differentiation of effective interest rates can mitigate the adverse selection problem. In the absence of group liability, an uninformed lender should offer a uniform interest rate to all borrowers, based on the average risk level; however, in such a case, the interest rate might be too high to attract safe borrowers. An advantage of peer screening is that a lender need not elicit local information (and thus incur investigation costs) in order to offer interest rates that differ by risk level.

Other important mechanisms suggested by theoretical studies are peer monitoring and peer enforcement. Once a group is formed, each borrower individually decides how to use his or her loan. Although some MFIs restrict the purpose of their loans to income-generating activities—such as productive investments—the loan can be diverted for any use, due to its fungibility. Regardless of the ultimate purpose of a loan, the borrower must exert efforts to keep his or her business performing in order to be able to make repayments successfully. If his or her inappropriate behavior in terms of the loan's purpose and effort levels leads to repayment failure, the burden of default should be borne by the other group members. Therefore, borrowers have an incentive to monitor each other and to pressure their peers into appropriate behaviors, as long as they can observe one another's actions. Peer monitoring mitigates an *ex ante* moral hazard problem—in the absence of the ability to observe borrowers' actions, a lender should use financial rewards and punishments, depending solely on the repayment results, to preclude an *ex ante* moral hazard. However, peer based group liability severely restricts the possibility of financial punishment. In this respect, the presence of non-financial social sanctions on which borrowers can rely is critical to punishing misbehavior. A similar scenario applies to the prevention of an *ex post* moral hazard problem. After income is realized, a borrower might have the opportunity to pocket his or her earnings and default on the loan, even though those earnings are sufficient to make a repayment. A lender cannot force such defaulting borrowers to repay, because the cost of verifying the income concerned is prohibitively high. Again, using local information and social pressure, group borrowers have an incentive to discourage peers from engaging in strategic defaults.

A basic presumption underlying the aforementioned peer mechanisms is the existence of social interaction among the group members, which makes it easier to observe one another's personalities and actions. In addition, borrowers are thought to be endowed with capabilities of enforcing social sanctions in cases of default by their fellow members. It is, therefore, interesting to ask whether strong social interaction among group members affects repayment performance under group liability lending. A handful of empirical studies examine this question (Wydick 1999; Ahlin and Townsend 2007; Karlan 2007). Using non-experimental data from Guatemala, Wydick (1999) concludes that previously existing social ties per se have little impact on repayment rates.[1] Ahlin and Townsend (2007) show that in Thailand, strong social ties have adverse impacts on repayment probability. This contradicts theoretical predictions. On the other hand, based on data from FINCA-Peru, Karlan (2007) finds evidence that social connections, measured in terms of geographical proximity and cultural similarity, increase peer monitoring and have a positive impact on high repayment rates. Because his study uses a quasi-experimental environment in which borrowers are randomly sorted into groups, any endogeneity problems arising from the possibility that social connections affect both the group-formation process and the economic opportunities should have been avoided. Cassar et al. (2007) also finds a positive relationship between social connections and repayment performance in South Africa and Armenia.

---

[1] Wydick finds that intensive monitoring and the willingness to punish misbehaviors are associated with high repayment rates. However, previously existing social ties are not necessarily prerequisites for the intensity of monitoring or strict enforcement.

Feigenberg et al. (2011) shed light on a different aspect of social interactions by comparing two types of randomly assigned groups. One is a group with weekly meetings, and the other has monthly meetings.[2] They found that more frequent meetings facilitate informal risk-sharing among the members. Clients who met on a weekly basis achieved higher repayment rates than clients who met on a monthly basis, even after all the groups were converted to the same frequency of group meetings. Overall, the empirical results suggest that the intensity of monitoring and the potential for social sanctions are positively related to lower rates of default. However, too-strong social ties can have adverse impacts on repayment rates, because close relationships among borrowers make them reluctant to inflict severe sanctions on their fellow members, even if doing so is optimal from the *ex ante* point of view. As a result, social interactions have both negative and positive effects on repayment performance. Positive effects may arise not just from improved monitoring and/or enforcement, but also from enhanced informal risk-sharing among borrowers.

As discussed, theoretical models of peer monitoring and peer enforcement have some empirical support. With regard to peer screening, Ahlin (2009) finds evidence for homogenous sorting, by risk level, in group liability lending in Thailand. Assortative matching and appropriate risk-pricing, as predicted by a peer-screening model, are empirically supported by the data. However, he also reveals the tendency for there to be a lack of diversification, vis-à-vis risk, within groups. This result indicates that a borrower tries to lower the chances of facing liability for fellow group members by choosing a similar type of business as the others. Therefore, peer screening may limit the scope of efficient risk-sharing among borrowers. Bryan et al. (2012) assessed whether peers have superior information on the creditworthiness of their friends and can use social pressure to enforce loan repayments. Instead of group liability, borrowers who are individually liable are given monetary incentives to screen their friends and enforce repayment. Experimental evidence from microcredit borrowers in South Africa shows that peers are effective in enforcing repayment, even when they have no more information on their friends than the lender does. The results of Bryan et al. indicate that the peer-screening mechanism is less effective in their study location. Finally, using observational data from Thailand, Ahlin and Townsend (2007) assess the relative importance of all the existing models. This unique challenge reveals that the peer enforcement model performs well in poor, low-infrastructure regions, and that the peer-screening model effectively explains the data in the more affluent region close to the capital city. Taken together, while each mechanism suggested by theory works in some specific contexts, there is no mechanism that works well universally. Furthermore, the relative importance of such mechanisms in practice depends on many location-specific factors, such as economic, cultural, and historical conditions.

[2] The clients in their experiment are on individual liability lending contracts, while groups are formed only for cost-saving reasons. The endogenous self-selection problem, therefore, is not a serious issue in their study.

2.2.2 Group Versus Individual Liability Lending

In 2002, the Grameen Bank introduced the so-called Grameen II system. Among other features, the Grameen II system formally eliminates group liability and allows for flexible repayment (Dowla and Barua 2006; Collins et al. 2009).[3] Individual liability lending is now increasingly popular among MFIs. For example, BancoSol, a large Bolivian MFI, has moved a large share of its portfolio to individual liability, and both Bank Rakyat Indonesia (BRI), a flagship MFI of Indonesia, and the ASA in Bangladesh have increased the number of loan clients who do not make use of group liability. Today, there are three major types of lending methodology available in the microcredit industry: group liability lending, individual liability lending, and FINCA-style village banking (Karlan and Mullainathan 2009). According to the Microfinance Information Exchange (2010) database, 37 % of the 972 MFIs worldwide exclusively adopt individual liability lending, while 44 % adopt both group and individual lending. Hence, group liability is not the sole lending methodology used today. On the contrary, group liability lending is becoming a smaller part of the overall portfolio of this growing industry.

Although individual liability lending can release borrowers from social pressure and attract a greater number of potential clients, an apparent concern is how a lender can enforce loan repayment in the absence of any peer mechanisms. What is important in this regard is that most MFIs retain other aspects of the classic Grameen model, even under individual lending. The classic features include regular group meetings, the contingent renewal of loans, forced savings and public and frequent repayment. Regular group repayment (without group liability) reduces administrative costs. The contingent renewal of loans should create dynamic incentives for borrowers to maintain good repayment records.[4] Forced savings works like an insurance mechanism to adjust the weekly repayment in case of income difficulties. Making repayment public imposes additional costs that defaulting borrowers incur due to a loss of reputation. Finally, frequent installments are believed to maintain repayment discipline and make it possible for credit officers to notice early evidence of problematic borrowers. Although these features have been combined with group liability in the classic model since the early days of microfinance, their roles have been overlooked by economists until recently.

In addition to an awareness of the potential benefits arising from several features other than group liability, economists also tend to pay greater attention to the potential costs of group liability lending. Fischer (2012) argues that group liability can cause distortions vis-à-vis the borrowers' investment choices. If information is imperfect and informal risk-sharing contract is incomplete, borrowers can

---

[3] At the same time, the Grameen Bank introduced new saving products to the market. I discuss the roles of savings and flexible repayment schedules in subsequent sections.

[4] In general, the amount of the renewed loan is greater than that of the previous cycle. This feature of progressive lending strengthens the effects of dynamic incentives.

"free ride" on their partners by taking risky but high-expected-return investments, without compensating their partners when risky investments generate very high returns. On the other hand, if information is perfect, peer approval of the project type will discourage borrowers from making excessively risky investments, thus also reducing expected returns. Group liability, therefore, leads to either an over- or under-investment in risky projects. Making too-safe investments under group liability lending is consistent with the empirical fact that the typical microfinance-funded business experiences only sluggish growth. Fischer conducted several lab experiments with actual microfinance borrowers in India and confirmed theoretical predictions that group liability discourages risky but high-expected-return investments.

Despite the increasing trend towards individual liability lending, direct, empirical comparisons between group and individual liability lending are surprisingly rare. The study of Giné and Karlan (2011) is a notable exception. They report on a field experiment in the Philippines in which some pre-existing groups were randomly converted from group to individual liability lending. They found there to be no change in repayment rates under individual liability lending. (Note that their experiment could not identify the effect of peer screening, because the converted groups were originally formed under group liability lending.) The findings of Carpena et al. (2013), vis-à-vis changes in liability structure, run completely counter to those of Giné and Karlan. Based on data from a natural experiment in India, they assessed the repayment impact of the conversion from individual to group liability lending, and they found there to be an *increase* in repayment rates under group liability lending. The results of these two studies seem to suggest that both group and individual liability lending perform equally well, as long as the screening of potential clients is successfully done under individual liability lending. In this respect, it seems that the role of investigations by credit officers is more important under individual liability lending than under group liability lending.

Group liability lending has played a considerable role in extending loan markets to the poor in developing countries. However, it is still unclear as to which theoretical mechanism truly works in practice, in various conditions. In addition, group liability and resulting social pressures impose an excessive burden on group borrowers within the system. Increasing attention is now being paid to other aspects of microcredit loans, including repayment frequency, dynamic incentives, and the issue of people's public reputation. Individual liability lending that features these elements is thought to be sustainable when the screening of potential clients does not become a serious issue. In the next section, I discuss further the role of repayment frequency, since it is a central factor that imposes excessive rigidity on microcredit loans.

2.3 Rigid and Flexible Repayment Rules

2.3.1 Repayment Frequency as a Commitment Device

Most microcredit loans require frequent repayment installments, either weekly or monthly, and repayment starts immediately following the disbursement of the loan. In addition, the amount of each repayment is fixed and usually non-negotiable during the repayment period. This rigid repayment schedule has been advocated by many microfinance professionals. Their argument is that it helps borrowers build their financial discipline and ability to save. Unless borrowers are obliged to make small installments regularly, they need to accumulate a certain amount of money to make a repayment at the end of the loan cycle. However, savings accumulation is sometimes difficult for the poor, because of savings constraints, sudden need expenditures, and the consumption of tempting goods.

Several pieces of empirical evidence point to the difficulties borrowers experience in saving (Ashraf et al. 2006; Gugerty 2007; Collins et al. 2009). This evidence has been interpreted along the lines of behavioral weakness and present-biased preferences (Laibson 1997). People are sometimes unable to resist immediate temptation, even if they value future consumption, and they end up with a smaller amount of savings than originally planned. In such cases, a rigid microfinance schedule with frequent repayments provides borrowers with opportunities to commit to savings-like behavior. Hence, if a potential borrower needs a loan and also desires not to default, rigid repayment rules have been found to be helpful for this borrower. Based on this sort of argument, Bauer et al. (2012) examined the relationship in India between behavioral weakness and participation in microfinance. Using data obtained from lab experiments in the field, they found that present-biased women are more likely to borrow from a local MFI to meet their loan demands. This result suggests that, when taking into account the behavioral aspects of clients, a rigid schedule with frequent repayments should be supported as a useful commitment device. Fischer and Ghatak (2010) provide another justification for the "frequent repayment" rule. They construct a theoretical model in which borrowers have present-biased preferences, and they show that under some conditions, frequent repayment both relaxes the constraints that come with repayment enforcement and increases the maximum incentive to take an appropriate size of loan.

Overall, the "frequent repayment" rule of MFIs can work as a commitment device: in practice, "frequent repayment" has almost the same meaning as "frequent savings." It can also improve the welfare of present-biased borrowers by enabling optimal consumption allocation from an *ex ante* viewpoint.

2.3.2 Need for a Flexible Repayment Rule

While a schedule that features frequent repayments can help borrowers commit to repaying and lead to better allocations for consumption, how frequently should repayments be made? This is an important empirical question. Field and Pande (2008) compare randomly assigned weekly repayment groups to monthly repayment groups. They found there to be no significant difference in the repayment rates between the two groups. Hence, weekly repayments may not be essential in providing an effective commitment device. These results indicate that it may be possible to reduce the costs related to weekly meetings, for both the MFIs and the borrowers, by adopting a more infrequent repayment schedule without worsening repayment performance.

A serious drawback of a rigid repayment schedule lies, however, in the fact that it is not state-contingent. It is often observed that seasonal variations in income in rural areas also cause seasonal variations in consumption (Khandker 2012). In addition, a borrower usually faces income uncertainty at times. Whether it happens predictably or unpredictably, income fluctuation is a pervasive phenomenon that makes it difficult to smooth consumption over time. MFIs have recently tried to introduce state-contingent repayment rules to mitigate problems that are associated with a mismatch between the pattern of repayment and borrowers' cash flows. Shoji (2010) found that allowing borrowers to reschedule their repayments during times of natural disaster in Bangladesh significantly reduced their reliance on informal money-lenders and enabled consumption-smoothing. The Bank for Agriculture and Agricultural Cooperation (BAAC) in Thailand also allows *ex post* loan renegotiation if borrowers face repayment difficulties due to flooding, a drought, or the like (CGAP/IFAD 2006). Loan repayments can be safely rescheduled if the shocks are readily observed by the lenders. A flexible repayment schedule will attract more clients who are facing income uncertainty but are afraid of a possible default when they encounter negative shocks.

As for seasonality, a direct solution would be to provide better opportunities for commitment savings. Clients should be offered an account of their commitment savings when the periodic income level is high, such as after a harvest season, and withdrawals should be allowed only during severe periods, such as in lean seasons. These arrangements would help the poor with present-biased preferences to mitigate seasonal variations in income to some extent. Another possible solution for microcredit loans is to allow the suspension of repayment during the low-income season. Confianza in Peru and Banco Los Andes ProCredit in Bolivia both offer loan products where repayments are set according to revenue flows (CGAP/IFAD 2006). Field et al. (2011) assessed the effect of two-month grace periods before repayments start on the investment choices of business enterprises. They found that postponing repayment enhances the long-term development of a business by allowing a larger investment during the initial periods. However, their findings also revealed that grace periods increase the variance of investment returns and, therefore, lead to high default rates. Although their study is not directly related to income fluctuation, it provides further evidence of the existence of costs stemming from repayment moratoria. A flexible repayment schedule enhances the potential of clients who suffer from income fluctuations. However, there exists a concern about the erosion of financial discipline. Which effect is stronger depends on location-specific factors and on details pertaining to contract design. Clearly, further research needs to be undertaken in order to attain a better understanding of the mechanisms by which a flexible repayment schedule would improve client welfare, which will be aimed in the research of this book.

2.4 Conclusion

Group liability and a fixed repayment schedule with frequent installments are prominent features of microcredit loan contracts. They make it possible for lenders to reduce lending costs and provide borrowers with appropriate incentives to repay. Sometimes they facilitate mutual insurance among members and improve the welfare of borrowers by providing a commitment device that induces saving-like behaviors. However, they also impose considerable burdens on borrowers.

MFIs have recently introduced more flexible loan products, such as individual liability loans and *ex post* negotiable loans with flexible repayment rules. Both empirical and theoretical studies indicate that flexibility within the terms of a lending contract has its costs and benefits; overall effects depend on location-specific factors and the actual design of flexible contracts. Seeking a better design for flexible loan contracts is beneficial to potential borrowers. The accumulation of empirical evidence also contributes to a better understanding of the conditions under which flexibility helps the poor while still preserving high repayment rates. Challenges with respect to the development of more flexible lending contracts persist, and further research efforts should be made in this fruitful area of exploration.

References

Ahlin C (2009) Matching for credit: risk and diversification in Thai Microcredit Groups. BREAD working paper no. 251

Ahlin C, Townsend R (2007) Using repayment data to test across models of joint liability lending. Econ J 117(517):1253–1267

Armendariz B, Morduch J (2010) The economics of microfinance, 2nd edn. MIT Press, Cambridge

Ashraf N, Karlan D, Yin W (2006) Tying odysseus to the mast: evidence from a commitment savings product in the Philippines. Q J Econ 121(2):635–672

Bauer M, Chytilova J, Morduch J (2012) Behavioral foundations of microcredit: experimental and survey evidence from rural India. Am Econ Rev (forthcoming)

Besley T, Coate S (1995) Group lending, repayment incentives and social collateral. J Dev Econ 46(1):1–18

Bryan G, Karlan D, Zinman J (2012) You can pick your friends, but you need to watch them: loan screening and enforcement in a referrals field experiment. Yale University mimeo

Cassar A, Crowley L, Wydick B (2007) The effect of social capital on group loan repayment: evidence from field experiments. Econ J 117(517):85–106

Carpena F, Cole S, Shapiro J, Zia B (2013) Liability structure in small-scale finance: evidence from a natural experiment. World Bank Econ Rev 27(3):437–469

CGAP/IFAD (2006) Managing risk and designing product for agricultural microfinance: features of an emerging model. Occasional paper 11

Collins D, Morduch J, Rutherford S, Ruthven O (2009) Portfolio of the poor: how the world's poor live on $2 a day. Princeton University Press

Dowla A, Barua D (2006) The poor always pay back: the Grameen II story. Kumarian Press

Feigenberg B, Field E, Pande R (2011) The economic returns to social interaction: experimental evidence from microfinance. Harvard University mimeo

Fischer G (2012) Contract structure, risk sharing, and investment choice. Econometrica (forthcoming)

Fischer G, Ghatak M (2010) Repayment frequency in microfinance contracts with present-biased borrowers. London School of Economics mimeo

Field E, Pande R (2008) Repayment frequency and default in micro-finance: evidence from India. J Eur Econ Assoc 6(2–3):501–509

Field E, Pande R, Papp J, Rigol N (2011) Term structure of debt and entrepreneurship: evidence from microfinance. Working paper

Ghatak M (1999) Group lending, local information and peer selection. J Dev Econ 60(1):27–50

Ghatak M, Guinnane TW (1999) The economics of lending with joint liability: theory and practice. J Dev Econ 60(1):195–228

Giné X, Karlan DS (2011) Group versus individual liability: short and long-term evidence from Philippine microcredit lending groups, June 2011. Yale University mimeo

Gugerty MK (2007) You can't save alone: commitment in rotating savings and credit associations in Kenya. Econ Dev and Cul Change 55(2):251–282

Karlan D (2007) Social connections and group banking. Econ J 117(517):52–84

Karlan D, Mullainathan S (2009) Rigidity in microfinancing: can one size fit all? QFINANCE. (http://www.qfinance.com/financing-best-practice/rigidity-in-microfinancing-can-one-size-fit-all?page=1)

Khandker SR (2012) Seasonality of income and poverty in Bangladesh. J Dev Econ 97:244–256

Kono H, Takahashi K (2010) Microfinance revolution: its effects, innovations, and challenges. Dev Econ 48(1):15–73

Laibson D (1997) Golden eggs and hyperbolic discounting. Q J Econ 112(2):443–478

Microfinance Information Exchange (2010) 2009 MFI Benchmarks. (http://www.themix.org/publications/microbanking-bulletin/2010/10/2009-mfi-benchmarks)

Shoji M (2010) Does contingent repayment in microfinance help the poor during natural disasters? J Dev Stud 46(2):191–210

Stiglitz JE (1990) Peer monitoring and credit markets. World Bank Econ Rev 4(3):351–366

Varian HR (1990) Monitoring agents with other agents. J Inst Theor Econ 146(1):153–174

Wydick B (1999) Can social cohesion be harnessed to repair market failures? Evidence from group lending in Guatemala. Econ J 109(457):463–475

Chapter 3
Seasonal Deprivation and Microcredit in Northern Bangladesh

Tatsufumi Yamagata

Abstract People in northwest Bangladesh face triple handicaps, i.e., floods, an agricultural lean season, and cold waves. The seasonal deprivation caused by the handicaps, called *monga* in Bengali, might be attenuated by microfinance if it reached people in need and supplied liquidity to ease their budget constraints. However, the prototype microfinance invented by Grameen Bank included a package of rules that are inharmonious with conditions in northwest Bangladesh. For instance, weekly repayments and attendance at weekly meetings are among the rules of the prototype microfinance. Seasonal floods and resulting seasonal deprivation make these conditions unrealistic. This chapter shows how Grameen Bank, PKSF and other microfinance institutions are attempting to address the rigidity of the prototype microfinance by adding various forms of flexibility in their contracts.

Keywords Northern Bangladesh · Microcredit · Seasonal deprivation

3.1 Introduction

People in northwest Bangladesh face triple handicaps, i.e., floods, an agricultural lean season, and cold waves. Floods force people to move from their residences for extended periods. Furthermore, flood damage is more severe for those who have nowhere to live but at the waterfront. The agricultural lean season after *Aman* paddy creates temporary joblessness and a famine-type situation as well as cold waves, which lower the temperature in the area and cause low yield of crops.

This seasonal deprivation, called *monga* in Bengali, might be attenuated by microfinance if it reached people in need and supplied liquidity to ease their

T. Yamagata (✉)
Institute of Developing Economies, Japan External Trade Organization (IDE-JETRO),
3-2-2, Wakaba, Mihama-ku, Chiba 261-8545, Japan
e-mail: tatsufumi_yamagata@ide.go.jp

A. S. Shonchoy (ed.), *Seasonality and Microcredit*, SpringerBriefs in Economics,
DOI: 10.1007/978-4-431-55010-5_3, © IDE-JETRO 2014

budget constraints. As detailed in the previous chapter, however, the prototype microfinance invented by Grameen Bank included a package of rules that are inharmonious with conditions in northwest Bangladesh. For instance, weekly repayments and attendance at weekly meetings are among the rules of the prototype microfinance (Morduch 1999a). However, seasonal floods and resulting seasonal deprivation make meeting these conditions unrealistic. People living in a flood-prone area have to escape from floods and live from hand to mouth during such times. Thus, this prototype microfinance does not work in such an area.

This contradiction between the prototype microfinance and living conditions in northwest Bangladesh is this study's point of departure. In this chapter, the living conditions and actual operation of microfinance in northwest Bangladesh are described before the following chapters elaborate upon the empirical analyses.

3.2 Seasonal Deprivation

3.2.1 Natural Conditions

Seasonal deprivation is remarkably acute in the Rangpur Division,[1] which consists of eight districts: Dinajpur, Gaibandha, Kurigram, Lalmonirhat, Nilphamari, Panchagarh, Rangpur, and Thakurgaon. Among these, Gaibandha and Kurigram are the most *monga*-prone because the Jamuna River[2] flows through them, causing local floods. A tributary of the Jamuna River, Teesta River, flows along the borders of Lalmonirhat, Nilphamari, Rangpur, Kurigram, and Gaibandha. Consequently, river basin areas in these districts are also affected by floods. However, as the Jamuna River is considerably wider than the Teesta River, its floods affect a greater area (Fig. 3.1).

The floods lead to the formation of islands made from silt, called *chars*. *Chars* are islands located within a river, formed by run-off soil. A *char* area is vulnerable to floods; however, for the sake of poor peasants, it is a frontier that no one claims to own,[3] and is useful for both farming and living. Moreover, there is ample fresh

[1] Rangpur Division was part of the Rajshahi Division before it separated in 2010 to form a new regional division. According to the terminology of geographical hierarchy with respect to local administration in Bangladesh, a division is a higher level of classification containing several districts. As of 2013, Bangladesh had seven divisions and 64 districts.

[2] The Jamuna River is a major tributary of the Brahmaputra River.

[3] Because of this "no man's land" nature, illegitimate occupation of certain parts and conflicts among occupants frequently occur on newly created *chars*. As for laws and institutional settings concerning *chars* and some case studies of livelihood, local administration, violence and political disputes, see Barkat et al. (2007). The same authors collected household data of people living in *chars* in five districts in Bangladesh: Noakhali, Pabna, Rajbari, Rajshahi, and Tangail. Noakhali is a district along the Bay of Bengal, whose seashore suffers from ocean erosion. Pabna, Rajbari, and Rajshahi face the Padma River, which is one of the three greatest rivers flowing into Bangladesh and

Fig. 3.1 Map of Bangladesh

(Footnote 3 continued)
which is the main branch of the Ganges River within Bangladesh. Tangail, which faces the Jamuna River on its western side, is a few hours' drive from Dhaka. None of the districts studied by Barkat et al. (2007) are affected by *monga*, which is seasonal deprivation, as described later.

water for agriculture. These three features are applicable to reclaimed land seasonally emerging from and submerging in river basins. Therefore, some peasants prefer to reside in a *char* area within a river basin to secure fertile and unoccupied land, even if it is for one crop cycle.

Char land, however, is inferior to river basin land in terms of networks and logistics. Reclaimed river basins have roads and communication connections with the other side of the river. However, the surrounding river water isolates *char* land from both riverbanks. The Jamuna River includes some *char* islands sizeable enough for people to live on for extended durations. The inconvenience and vulnerability of a *char* island is aggravated by factors such as its distance from the mainland, its small size, and a lack of hills. *Char* islands are not connected to electricity or land telecommunications networks. Electricity is available only through in-house power generation using fuel or solar energy. Meanwhile, big *char* islands might have schools, emergency evacuation centers, and other minor community level facilities.

The natural hardships faced by northwest Bangladesh are partially reflected in the region's temperatures. Figures 3.2 and 3.3 display average temperature recorded by month in 2009 and 2010, respectively, at meteorological stations in Dhaka and Rangpur. Both figures show monthly averages of daily maximum and minimum temperatures in Rangpur,[4] while Dhaka's temperatures are included for reference.

These figures clearly indicate that Rangpur's monthly average minimum temperature was always lower than Dhaka's in both 2009 and 2010. Furthermore, December and January are the coldest months. In Rangpur, monthly average minimum temperatures were below 15 °C in 2009. The average temperature in January 2010 was 10.5° (Fig. 3.3). Since Figs. 3.2 and 3.3 show monthly averages of daily maximum and minimum temperatures, variation around the average obviously exist. That is, the January 2010 average minimum temperature of 10.5° implies that the minimum temperatures on some dates were below 10.5°. People laboring or living outdoors without sufficient clothing in such temperatures will certainly suffer from the cold.

Another aspect of temperature that deserves special mention also concerns Rangpur, where the daily maximum temperature during the second half of the year reaches the same highs as it does in Dhaka. In November and December 2009, the monthly averages of daily maximum temperature in both Rangpur and Dhaka were over 30°, while Rangpur's minimum temperature in December 2009 was below 15°. Thus, the difference between maximum and minimum temperatures was as great as 18.4°. In November and December 2010, the monthly averages of daily maximum temperature declined to below 30° in Rangpur. Nevertheless, they remained as high as those in Dhaka.

---

[4] Rangpur neighbors both Gaibandha and Kurigram.

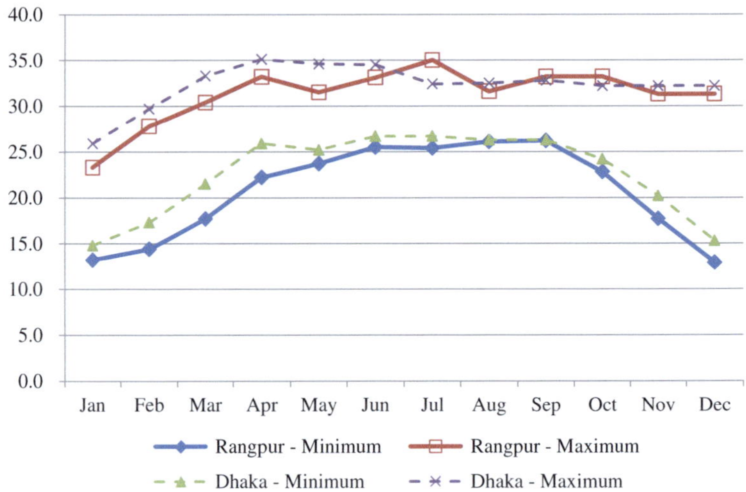

Fig. 3.2 Daily maximum and minimum temperatures in Rangpur and Dhaka in 2009 (centigrade). *Source* BBS (2011)

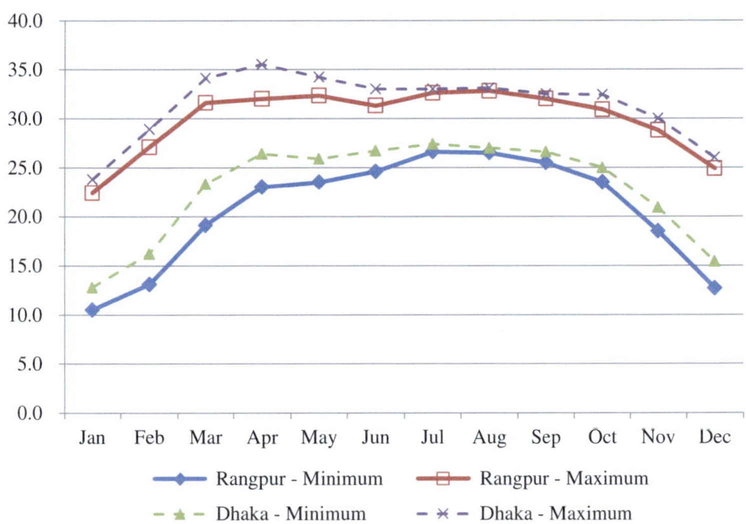

Fig. 3.3 Daily maximum and minimum temperatures in Rangpur and Dhaka in 2010 (*Unit* centigrade). *Source* BBS (2011)

Therefore, since Rangpur is located inland, similar to other parts of northwest Bangladesh, its climate is more continental. That is, temperatures are high during the day and low at night. Thus, acclimatizing to these extremes can be highly difficult for those living in Rangpur as well as other parts of northwest Bangladesh.

3.2.2 Poverty

Before Jamuna Bridge was built over the Jamuna River between Tangail and Sirajganj Districts in 1998, northwest Bangladesh was not well connected to any major city in the country. There were few paved roads, and the region's economy heavily depended on water transportation down the Jamuna River. Roads that did exist were easily damaged by sunshine, rainfall, and traffic. Thus, logistics to and from northwest Bangladesh were generally unfavorable, economic activity was static, and the economy was vulnerable to both natural and man-made risks.

Therefore, the region's standard of living has long been low. As mentioned above, in addition to the seasonal lean period, two natural factors put the region's economy at a disadvantage, i.e., floods and cold waves. Given the combined effect of these adverse conditions, the overall level of agricultural production has been so low that the region's food stocks are unlikely to be sufficient between harvest seasons. Bangladesh's staple crop is rice, with three main types that grow in different seasons: *Aus* (December/January–March), *Boro* (March/April–June/July), and *Aman* (July/August–November/December).[5] Thus, after August, people must wait until December for the next harvest. As a result, there is generally a food shortage from September to November,[6] which is known as *monga* in Bengali.

Monga symbolizes poverty in northwest Bangladesh. This cyclical food insecurity causes many residents from the region to migrate to Dhaka and nearby cities such as Bogra. In particular, *char* islands, widespread in Gaibandha and Kurigram, are isolated from the mainland, and education, jobs, entertainment, and public utilities are rarely available on them.

Khandker (2012) uses samples from the Household Income and Expenditure Surveys (HIES) conducted in 2000 and 2005 to reveal that income reductions experienced during *monga* periods did not get smoothed out, while consumption also declines during *monga* owing to imperfections of the financial market in the greater Rangpur region[7] as well as in the rest of Bangladesh. In addition, this study shows that drops in consumption and income are more distinct in the greater Rangpur region than in the rest of Bangladesh.

HIES also highlight overall poverty in northwest Bangladesh. Figures 3.4 and 3.5 display the incidence of poverty in 2000 and 2005 measured by division with head count ratio. Note that Rangpur Division, which separated from Rajshahi Division in 2010, was included in the latter in these figures.

---

[5] See Khandker (2012: 245), Khandker and Mahmud (2012: 33–64), Rahman et al. (2009: 95–98) for more details.

[6] A Bengali month called *Kartik*, running from mid-October to mid-November, lies in the lean season. *Kartik* is therefore referred to as *Mora Kartik*, the dying month. See Rahman et al. (2009: 95–98) for more details. Also see Ahmed et al. (2009: 271–273) on *monga*.

[7] In his terminology, the "greater Rangpur region" comprises four districts: Gaibandha, Kurigram, Lalmonirhat, and Nilphamari.

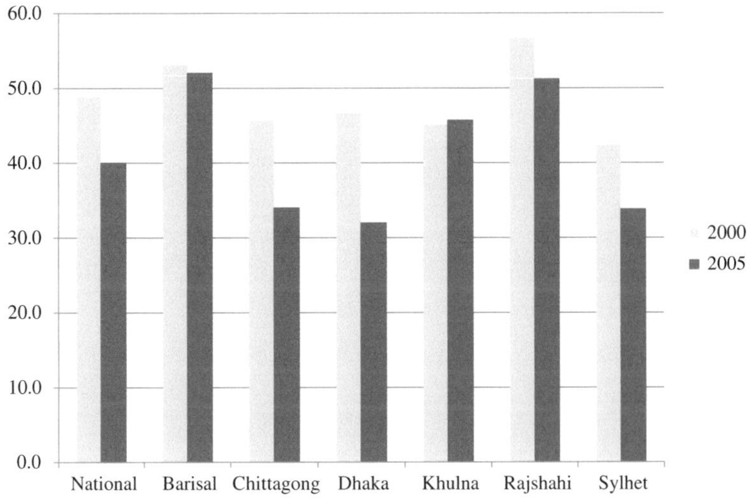

Fig. 3.4 Incidence of poverty with upper poverty line. *Source* BBS (2010), Table 14.23

Using upper poverty lines, which are more frequently cited than lower poverty lines, the incidence of poverty in Bangladesh as a whole was 48.9 % in 2000. The divisions exhibiting higher incidence of poverty than the national average are Rajshahi and Barisal, which belong to the south of Bangladesh, an area susceptible to cyclones from the Bay of Bengal.

From 2000 to 2005, the incidence of poverty in Bangladesh dropped from 48.9 to 40.0 %. Thus, some poverty reduction was achieved throughout the country; however, it was not equal across all divisions. Divisions having lower poverty in 2000, such as Dhaka, Chittagong, and Sylhet, further reduced its incidence by 2005, while those with higher levels in 2000, such as Barisal, Rajshahi, and Khulna, did not achieve the same degree of poverty reduction. More concretely, from 2000 to 2005, the incidence of poverty in Barisal and Rajshahi declined by only 1.1 and 5.5 percentage points, respectively. In Khulna, poverty even increased by 0.6 percentage points. At the same time, poverty declined in Dhaka and Chittagong Divisions by 14.7 and 11.7 points, respectively.

This tendency of polarization is demonstrated in Fig. 3.5, where a lower poverty line is used. The lower poverty line allows severe poverty to be highlighted. Poverty declined throughout Bangladesh and in Dhaka and Chittagong Divisions by 9.2, 14.6, and 11.4 percentage points, respectively, while it decreased in Rajshahi and Khulna Divisions by 8.2 and 0.7 percentage points, respectively. On the other hand, poverty in Barisal District increased by 0.9 percentage points. Thus, poverty reduction in Rajshahi Division has been modest, a pattern also seen in other low-income divisions.

Incidence of poverty, measured via head count ratio, is an insensitive indicator of poverty in that the ratio does not reflect small changes in income by the very low income segment of the poor. Therefore, head count ratio is supplemented by

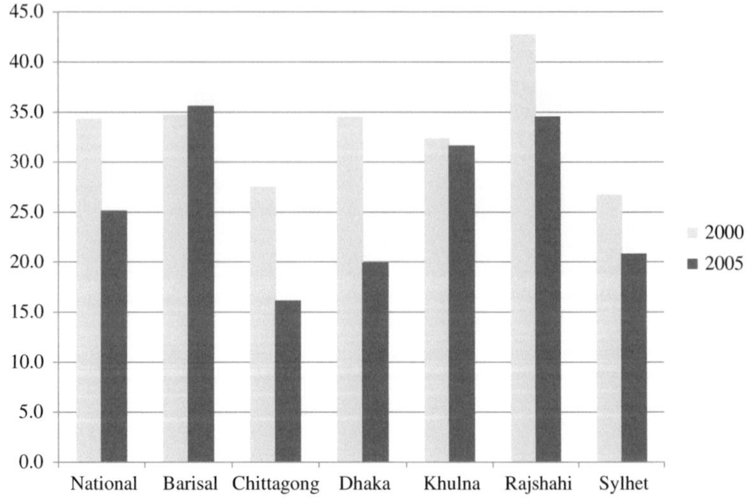

Fig. 3.5 Incidence of poverty with lower poverty line. *Source* BBS (2010), Table 14.23

other poverty indicators such as poverty gap ratio, which incorporates depth of poverty. Moreover, the squared poverty gap ratio is invoked to place greater emphasis on changes in income of the most poor.[8]

With upper and lower poverty lines, Figs. 3.6 and 3.7 show poverty gap ratios and squared poverty gap ratios by Division for 2010. Note that Rangpur Division separated from Rajshahi Division in 2010, making Rajshahi Division smaller.

Poverty gap ratios are outstandingly high in Barisal and Rangpur Divisions in 2010,[9] regardless of which poverty line is used (Fig. 3.6). Poverty gap ratios in Barisal and Rangpur are around 10 % with upper poverty lines, while those in other divisions are 4–6 %. Similar polarization appears in the poverty gap ratio with lower poverty lines. General inclinations by divisions hold even with squared poverty gap ratios (Fig. 3.7).

Finally, we examine an aspect of non-income poverty, education. Table 3.1 displays the literacy rate by region among people over seven years old by using data derived from the 2001 population census. The adult literacy rate in Bangladesh as a whole was 46.15 % in 2001. Literacy rates in two metropolises, Dhaka and Chittagong Districts, were higher than the national average. It is impressive that literacy

---

[8] For the details of poverty indicators, refer to Deaton (1997), and Haughton and Khandker (2009). A seminal study on this issue is Foster et al. (1984).

[9] Some information derived from the Household Income and Expenditure Survey (HIES) in 2010 appears in Bangladesh Bureau of Statistics (2011; BBS). Though the poverty gap ratio and squared poverty gap ratio by division derived from HIES 2010 are exhibited in BBS (2011), the head count ratio from HIES 2010 is not shown. Therefore, only the poverty gap ratio and squared poverty gap ratio in 2010 are given in this chapter.

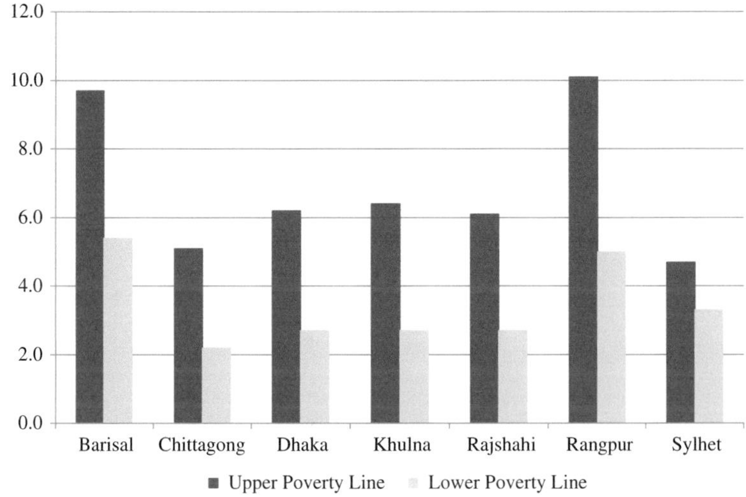

Fig. 3.6 Poverty gap ratio in 2010. *Source* BBS (2011), Table 14.25

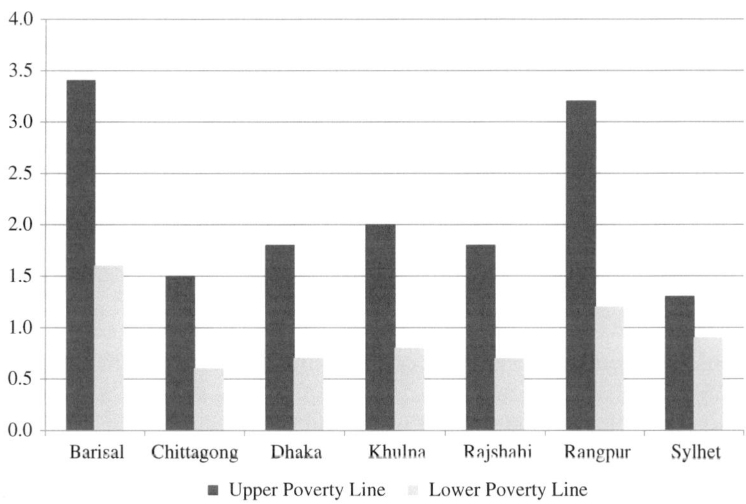

Fig. 3.7 Squared poverty gap ratio in 2010. *Source* BBS (2011), Table 14.25

in Barisal, the poorest division after Rangpur, is 53.59 %, considerably higher than the national average.

By contrast, the literacy rate in Rajshahi Division is remarkably lower than the national average. In Rajshahi Division, Gaibandha and Kurigram Districts exhibit very low literacy rates, with only a third of the population able to read and write. This level is significantly lower than not only the national average but also the average in Rajshahi Division.

Table 3.1 Adult literacy ratio by division and district in 2001 (percentage)

Division/district	Literacy rate
Whole Bangladesh	46.15
Barisal division	53.59
Chittagong division	47.89
Chittagong district	50.29
Dhaka division	43.59
Dhaka district	47.10
Khulna division	48.62
Rajshahi division	41.81
Rajshahi district	47.54
Rangpur district	41.91
Gaibandha district	35.73
Kurigram district	33.45
Sylhet division	40.33

Note children younger than seven years old are not counted when calculating the literacy rate
Source the original source of the literacy rate is *Population Census* 2001, while the literacy figures were cited from BBS (2011)

As detailed in the next chapter, Gaibandha and Kurigram Districts are the geographical areas featured in this book. These districts are highly susceptible to floods and *mongas*. Consequently, they suffer poverty on both income and non-income grounds.

3.3 Microfinance

Microfinance first emerged in Chittagong. In 1976, Muhammad Yunus, the founder of Grameen Bank, commenced microfinance operations in a village near Chittagong University, where he taught (Yunus and Jolis 1998). Since then, microfinance spread first to other areas in Bangladesh, then to other organizations, and it is now present across the globe (Khandker 1998; Armendáriz de Aghion and Morduch 2005; Morduch 1999a).

However, microfinance did not spread at an even speed across regions. Areas suffering from physical disadvantages such as remoteness from main cities, insufficient transportation and communication infrastructure, and inhospitable natural conditions have difficulties absorbing microfinance institutions. Rangpur Division is one such area; thus, microfinance institutions rarely reach northwest Bangladesh.

Due to floods and *mongas*, people living in *chars* and river basins are highly mobile during both flood and *monga* seasons; this enables them to escape from floodwaters and find income-generating opportunities. Therefore, some important rules for the prototype microfinance practice are not feasible.

Since microfinance does not require collateral, another inducement to repay the loan is required. To motivate borrowers to repay regularly, prototype microfinance involves weekly meeting at which loan repayments are made. Moreover, weekly loan repayments begin almost immediately after the money is first lent. An ordinary loan contract allows a grace period that allows the borrower to invest and earn returns. Prototype microfinance, however, does not allow this grace period, instead prioritizing habituation of weekly repayment (Armendáriz de Aghion and Morduch 2005; Morduch 1999a). Thus, punctuality and regularity of repayment emerged as core principles of prototype microfinance.

However, these principles conflict with the ways of life of poor people in northwest Bangladesh, who are likely to be forced to relocate in order to escape from floods or chase income-generating opportunities. Therefore, the rules associated with weekly meetings may not be enforced.

How do microfinance institutions address this regional adversity? Some take special measures or participate in a special scheme to fill the gap between the prototype rules and reality. Some utilize countermeasures and behave as they do elsewhere. In the rest of this section, microfinance institutions are classified and their responses to hardships in implementing prototype microfinance rules are summarized.

3.3.1 Nationwide Organizations

Some sufficiently famous nationwide organizations can raise funds in their own name, such as Grameen Bank, BRAC, and ASA. They secure loans and grants both locally and globally[10] and extend their services nationwide. They have certain principles and policies that are upheld throughout the country by branch offices. In principle, they are independent of the Government of Bangladesh,[11] and they are formally registered as an NGO or bank.

Grameen Bank is the pioneer of microfinance. The word *Grameen* is an adjective of *gram*, meaning "village" in Bengali. Established by Muhammad Yunus, the bank has introduced microfinance to the rest of the world. A main feature of its style of microfinance is group lending, associated with peer selection, peer monitoring, and joint liability (Morduch 1999a: 1580–1582). Joint liability means that if a group member is unable to make a complete repayment, the rest of the group is obliged to make the remainder of the repayment. A five-member

---

[10] According to an investigation by Morduch (1999b), subsidies play a great role in Grameen Bank. The same is true for most microfinance institutions. From this viewpoint, they are not pure commercial banks. However, as long as fund raisers consider their activities meaningful and are willing to continuously provide subsidies, the microfinance institution can be operated stably and soundly.

[11] Specifically, the Government of Bangladesh provides part of the capital (6 %, according to Grameen Bank's website), which caused Yunus' forced retirement by the government in 2011.

group is spontaneously generated through peer selection; therefore, a person inclined to default is likely to be ruled out. As a result, the ultra-poor, who face persistent difficulties in income generation, are unlikely to be able to obtain financial services from this style of microfinance. Thus, prototype Grameen-style microfinance is considered unable to reach the ultra-poor (Morduch 1999a: 1610).

In light of this penetration failure, Grameen Bank overhauled its original style of management and initiated another method of microfinance, "Grameen Bank II," in 2002 (Armendáriz de Aghion and Morduch 2005: 113). The Grameen Bank II scheme was designed to weaken the original framework's rigidity in several ways. First, the maturity of a new borrower's loan became flexible for periods ranging from 3 months to 3 years, a style dubbed "Easy Loans." Second, if a borrower with an Easy Loan faces repayment difficulties, another loan for a smaller amount, called a "Flexible Loan," is offered to get the Easy Loan back on track. The weekly repayment practice is retained. Thus, even the pioneering microfinance institution faces challenges in improving its management to better serve the ultra-poor.

BRAC was established by Fazle Hasan Abed in 1972 to help people displaced by the war for independence from Pakistan (Khandker 1998; Lovell 1992). BRAC claims to be the largest NGO in the world in terms of number of employees. By covering a wide geographical area through its activities, BRAC became the greatest microfinance provider in Bangladesh as of 2003.[12]

BRAC is known as an "integrated provider" of services, including more thansimply microfinance (Armendáriz de Aghion and Morduch 2005: 20; Khandker 1998: 16–17). After its emergency relief phase, BRAC's activities stressed skill development for the poor. Following Grameen Bank's success in microfinance, BRAC added rural credit to its skill-development program. According to Khandker (1998: 17),

> Over time BRAC and Grameen Bank have learned from one another. BRAC has learned that credit must be provided along with skills development training; Grameen Bank has realized that credit alone is not enough, that the poor need social development and organizational inputs to become more disciplined and productive.

BRAC's traditional emphasis on the importance of skill development remains alive. In 2002, BRAC launched a multidimensional microfinance program targeting the ultra-poor (Khandker and Mahmud 2012: 153). This program combines skill development, microfinance, and asset transfer, and the transferred assets include livestock and land for farming.

ASA's approach is contrary to BRAC's. ASA was founded by Shafiqual Haque Choudhury in 1978 as the Association for Social Advancement. Its acronym, ASA, meaning "hope" in Bengali, became its formal name. In 1991, ASA initiated

---

[12] According to the 2011 annual reports of BRAC and Grameen Bank, BRAC had 5.2 million active borrowers (BRAC 2011: 28), while Grameen Bank had 6.58 million. For the figure for Grameen Bank, see the following website: http://www.grameen-info.org/index.php?option=com_content&task=view&id=632&Itemid=664.

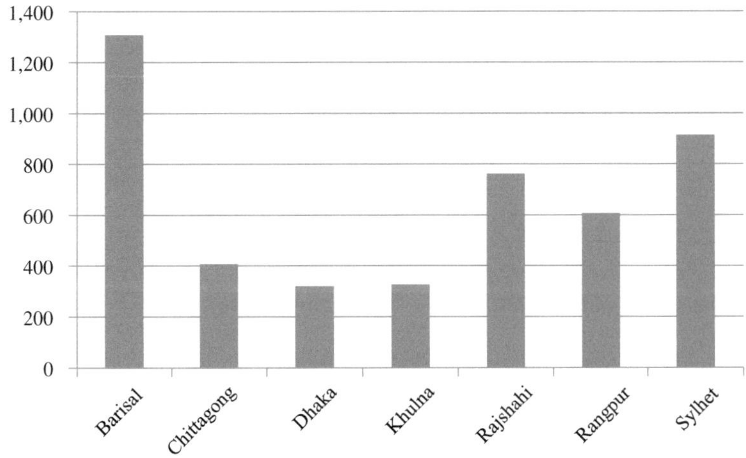

Fig. 3.8 Grameen bank's loan disbursement per person by district through the end of 2011 (in BDT). *Note* the figures were calculated by the author. *Original data* Grameen Bank (2011)

microfinance with the same features as Grameen Bank, i.e., group lending, but with a larger group, i.e., 20 people rather than five.

ASA's distinction lies in its pursuit of efficiency. While Grameen Bank had multiple types of loans such as general loans, housing loans, collective loans, and seasonal loans, ASA offered only one loan type and streamlined both record keeping and operations (Morduch 1999a: 1591). As a result of its pursuit of further efficiency, ASA stopped group lending and finally engaged in "individual lending." Even though the joint liability feature, previously regarded as a core principle of microfinance, was dropped, ASA's repayment rate was not sacrificed (Armendáriz de Aghion and Morduch 2005: 14).

Serving as a new model of microfinance, ASA's microfinance is now replicated in Ghana, India, Nigeria, Pakistan, and the Philippines. Grameen Bank was also motivated by ASA when it designed Grameen Bank II (Armendáriz de Aghion and Morduch 2005: 119–120). Thus, ASA established a global reputation vis-à-vis Grameen Bank and BRAC.

These nationwide organizations have several branches in northwest Bangladesh. However, their branches are rarely located in *chars* and flood-prone river basin areas, probably because nationwide organizations are less attuned to regional situations and affairs. According to the authors' casual conversation with officers and borrowers of Grameen Bank, the nationwide organization faces difficulty in holding weekly meetings in Gaibandha and Kurigram Districts. In fact, the low intensity of Grameen Bank's activities in northwest Bangladesh is reflected by the loan disbursement per capita by district. Figure 3.8 shows amounts until the end of 2011. Barisal District has seen the greatest growth in loans from Grameen Bank, while relatively rich districts, i.e., Chittagong, Dhaka, and Khulna, received less. These trends are understandable from the viewpoint of microfinance organizations' needs. However,

Rangpur District received significantly less than did Barisal, despite having similar poverty indicators. It also received less than two richer districts, Rajshahi and Sylhet. This contrast reveals that nationwide microfinance institutions face hardships in extending their services to Rangpur District.

3.3.2 Local NGOs and PKSF

In Bangladesh, more than 2000 NGOs are registered with the NGO Affairs Bureau of the Prime Minister's Office. Most are local NGOs established by local people with small funds. They conduct useful activities in their locality once the required resources are obtained.

Observing the successes of Grameen Bank, BRAC, ASA, and other NGOs in microfinance, in 1990, the Government of Bangladesh established Palli Karma-Sahayak Foundation (PKSF),[13] a "not-for-profit" company providing funds for microfinance to local NGOs. In addition to generating its own funds, PKSF attains funds from various sources including the Government of Bangladesh, the World Bank, the Asian Development Bank, the European Union, the International Fund for Agricultural Development, and the Department for International Development (DfID) of the United Kingdom. PKSF organizes various programs and projects, to which each donor contributes (PKSF 2011).

As of 2011, PKSF had 236 partner organizations throughout the country. These organizations participate in programs and projects and receive funds for activities such as microfinance. One such program focusing on *mongas* and floods in northwest Bangladesh is the Programmed Initiatives for *Monga* Eradication (PRIME), which is attached to the Learning and Innovation Fund to Test New Ideas (LIFT). Both were launched by PKSF in 2006 with funds provided by the DfID. Local NGOs applied to PRIME and LIFT to participate and attain funds for the programs.

PRIME consists of (1) flexible microfinance services, (2) promotion of income-generating activities, (3) technical training and services, (4) remittance services for domestic migration, (5) primary health care and additional interventions exclusively offered in lean season, (6) emergency loans, and (7) cash for local infrastructure development. Above all, (1) flexible microfinance and (6) emergency loans are core components. By receiving funds from PKSF, local NGOs with weak financial foundations can afford to conduct microfinance in northwest Bangladesh, where microfinance had previously been rare. LIFT provides funds for developing income-generating activities that are viable in northwest Bangladesh and that might be replicated by PRIME beneficiaries after it becomes feasible and profitable (PKSF 2009: 11; Khalily and Latif 2010: 22–37).

[13] Palli Karma-Sahayak Foundation means "Rural Activity Helping Foundation" in Bengali. There is no formal name of PKSF in English, though.

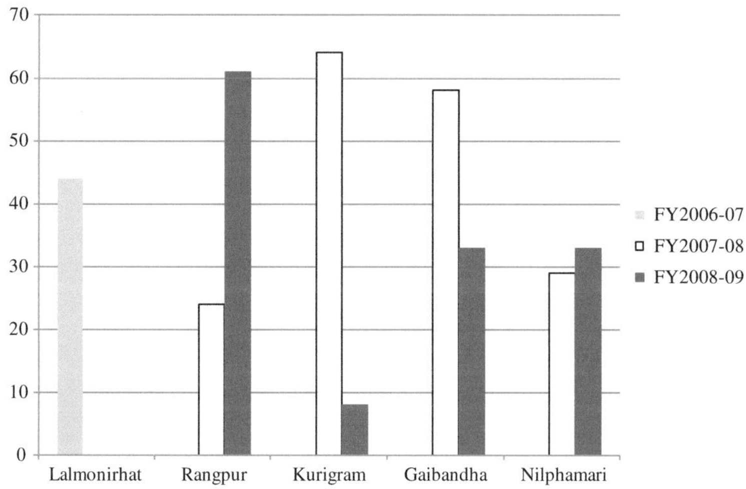

Fig. 3.9 Number of unions covered by PRIME's partner organizations by district. *Source* PKSF (2009: 15)

PRIME's first operation was conducted in FY2006–07 in Lalmonirhat District (which has a partial border along the Teesta River) in Rangpur Division with six partner organizations: Assistance for Social Organization and Development (ASOD), Eco-Social Development Organization (ESDO), Rangpur Dinajpur Rural Service (RDRS), Padakkhep Manobik Unnayan Kendra (PMUK: Centre for Sustained Human Development), People's Oriented Programme Implementation (POPI), and Thengamara Mohila Sabuj Sangha (TMSS).[14] These six organizations were already engaged in activities in Lalmonirhat District when they were selected as partner organizations for PRIME.

In FY2007–08, the program site was expanded to other districts in Rangpur Division: Rangpur, Kurigram, Gaibandha, and Nilphamari, as shown in Fig. 3.9. In this fiscal year, Kurigram and Gaibandha, through which the Jamuna River runs, were focal districts for extension. The following year, Unions[15] in Rangpur District, which is affected by the Teesta River, were prioritized.

In FY2007–08, five new partner organizations joined: Gram Unnayan Karma,[16] Gono Sastha Kendra (GSK),[17] United Development Initiatives for Programmed Actions (UDDIPAN), Society for Social Services (SSS), and Samaj Kallyan

[14] TMSS does not have any formal name in English. The name means "Thengamara Women-Youth Society." Thengamara is the village in which TMSS initiated its activity.

[15] Union is an administrative unit under Upazila, which is under district (alias, Zila). For example, Gaibandha District has 7 Upazilas, 82 Unions and 1,244 villages.

[16] This organization does not seem to have any formal name in English. The name means "Village Development Service."

[17] The name of this organization may be translated as "People's Health Center."

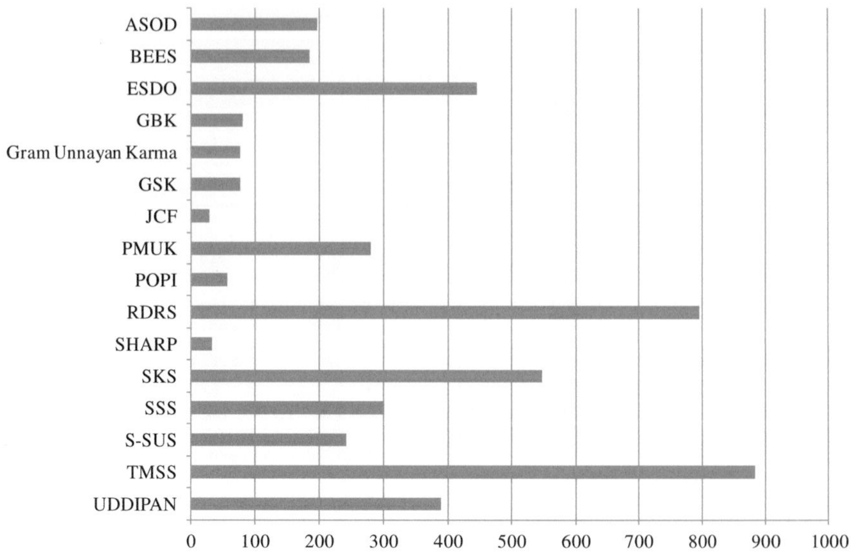

Fig. 3.10 Number of villages participating in PRIME by partner organization. *Source* PKSF (2009: 14)

Sangstha (SKS).[18] All have activities in either Gaibandha or Kurigram. In FY2008–09, five further organizations were added: Samakal Samaj Unnayan Sangstha (S-SUS),[19] Self-Help and Rehabilitation Program (SHARP), Gram Bikash Kendra (GBK),[20] Bangladesh Extension Education Services (BEES), and Jagoroni Chakra Foundation (JCF).[21]

Among the 16 partner organizations, TMSS works in the highest number of villages under PRIME (19.1 % of all villages under PRIME), followed by RDRS (17.2 %) (see Fig. 3.10). Other main contributors to PRIME are SKS (11.9 %), ESDO (9.6 %), and UDDIPAN (8.4 %). These organizations are local NGOs that have headquarters in Rangpur or Rajshahi District. According to this author's casual observation, microfinance in northwest Bangladesh is undertaken either through nationwide microfinance institutions or NGOs gaining funds from PKSF via PRIME.

Under the PRIME scheme, each partner organization formulates groups of beneficiaries in its geographical areas of longstanding activity. A group ranges from 25 to 30 persons. A partner organization offers these groups "flexible

[18] This may be translated as "Community Welfare Organization."

[19] This may be translated as "Contemporary Community Development Organization."

[20] This may be translated as "Village Development Center."

[21] *Jagoroni* may mean "awakening," while *chakra* means "wheel." Chakra has multiple connotations such as a spinning wheel, which Mahatma Gandhi used as a symbol of the Indian independence movement, and a center of vital energy in yoga terminology.

microfinance," in which loan amount, repayment schedule and frequency, as well as place of meeting are negotiable. At the same time, technical training and consultation regarding the microfinance's purpose are given to borrowers. In addition, supplementary services such as assistance for remittance among family members and primary health care are provided. Furthermore, in *monga* periods, emergency loans and employment opportunities for 100 days are offered if necessary (PKSF 2009: 9–32).

The advantages of PRIME's flexible microfinance over standard microfinance can be summarized as follows:

(1) Flexible loan amounts (the reference amount for the first loan to a beneficiary is BDT 4,000).
(2) Flexible repayment schedule.
(3) Flexible frequency and flexible place of meeting.
(4) Low interest rate equal to or below 10 %.
(5) No savings requirement and convenient savings withdrawal.
(6) Exemption from admission fee to the ultra-poor.

A feature of the PRIME scheme is that flexibilities in terms of amount, repayment schedule, and frequency of meeting are independently decided and hinge on negotiation between partner organization and beneficiaries. While this is ideal for beneficiaries, it is not easy to evaluate flexibility in terms of which aspect contributes to improvement of accessibility for microfinance beneficiaries; their performance in income-generating activities; and eventually, their family livelihood. Khalily and Latif (2010) and Khandker et al. (2010) have examined PRIME's impacts and found positive consequences, e.g., in outreach to the ultra-poor and seasonal-poor, reduction of seasonal deprivation and extreme poverty (Khandker et al. 2010), frequency of meals, and accumulation of assets such as livestock and land (Khalily and Latif 2010).

A research question in this book concerns which aspects of microfinance flexibility truly contribute to poverty reduction and social enhancement in north-west Bangladesh. As mentioned above, the PRIME scheme combines several aspects of flexibility, with the exact combination determined by the partner organization and borrower. In addition, such details of contracts between a partner organization and borrower are not documented as a form of statistical data.[22] To identify the aspects of flexibility that are important in addressing risks caused by *mongas* and floods as well as steps to mitigate the risk, it is necessary to treat flexibility in amount, repayment schedule, and frequency of meeting separately. This separation is undertaken by the authors of this book.

---

[22] Such details may be available on contracts between partner organizations and their beneficiaries. However, Khalily and Latif (2010) and Khandker et al. (2010) did not use a data set that identifies what aspects of flexibility truly applied to each borrower.

3.3.3 Gana Unnayan Kendra

For this study, our team selected Gana Unnayan Kendra (GUK)[23] as the partner organization. The name means "People's Development Center," though no formal English name is given. GUK was established in 1985 by the organization's chief executive, M. Abdus Salam. He was born in Gaibandha and initiated this organization to develop his native area, which faces chronic problems of *mongas* and floods caused by the Jamuna River. GUK is mainly funded by international donors such as Oxfam, DfID, the European Union, and NETZ Germany. Domestic sponsors include Ain O Salish Kendra[24] and the Centre for Disability in Development. Each sponsor has its own program with funds, which is undertaken by GUK as a partner organization. Therefore, all GUK activities are closely linked with their respective sponsors. This is a common method of local NGO management in Bangladesh.

GUK had 872 staff as of 2009, and it has five district offices, 17 *Upazila* offices, and 39 area offices. It has activities in *chars* in Gaibandha and Kurigram Districts. The Disaster Risk Reduction and Vulnerable Livelihoods Programme, funded by Oxfam Great Britain, and the Chars Livelihoods Programme (CLP), funded by DfID and the Australian Agency for International Development (AusAID), cover *chars* and river basins for livelihood enhancement through asset transfers involving cows, goats, and poultry. Hence, GUK is familiar with life in *monga*- and flood-prone areas. GUK owns a speedboat that connects the head office in Nashratpur, Gaibandha to Rajibpur Upazila, the southern tip of Kurigram, by a 2-h trip.

GUK had not included microfinance among its activities until our team approached it in 2010. It did not borrow money from PKSF and did not participate in PRIME. These two conditions, i.e., (1) rich experience of activities in *chars* and *monga*-prone areas and (2) non-participation in microfinance, were ideal for our team to conduct a randomized controlled trial on flexible microfinance because the control groups of borrowers do not have previous experience with standard microfinance, enabling the study team to begin both standard and flexible microfinance from scratch. At the same time, GUK has a firm organizational structure, many highly motivated staff members, and rich and extensive experience of working with international donors. On the basis of these viewpoints, our team selected GUK as the partner organization for implementing both standard and flexible microfinance.

---

[23] Gram Unnayan Karma, which is a partner organization of PRIME and which has its headquarters in Bogra District, also uses GUK as its acronym. In addition, another NGO named Gram Unnayan Kendra, meaning "Village Development Center," also uses the same acronym. Gram Unnayan Kendra's headquarters are located in Chilmari, Kurigram, and it is a partner organization of PKSF. However, throughout this book, GUK is used as an acronym for Gana Unnayan Kendra.

[24] No formal English name is given. The name may be translated as "Law and Arbitration Center."

3.4 Concluding Remarks

This chapter provided basic information on natural conditions, livelihood, and microfinance in northwest Bangladesh. Seasonal food insecurity and floods aggravate poverty in this area and prevent standard microfinance from working as it does in other parts of the country.

Microfinance may have potential to mitigate negative consequences from the seasonal deprivation and floods. To tap this potential, some flexibility must be allowed to deviate from the standard practices of microfinance developed by Grameen Bank. PKSF designed PRIME and allowed local NGOs to add flexibility, and its impact appears generally favorable. However, the particular aspects of flexibility that were critical for the favorable impact remain unknown, because full discretion was given to borrowers and partner organizations concerning how flexibility was incorporated into their contracts.

Therefore, a randomized controlled trial is necessary to identify the sources of flexibility contributing to favorable impacts and to determine policy implication in terms of the nature of flexibility that should be incorporated in standard microfinance. Empirical analyses presented in later chapters will elucidate these points.

References

Ahmed SS, Narayan A, Zaman H (2009) Are the poor protected?: vulnerability and the role of safety nets. In: Narayan A, Zaman H (eds) Breaking down poverty in Bangladesh. University Press Limited, Dhaka, pp 263–300

Armendáriz de Aghion B, Morduch J (2005) The economics of microfinance. MIT Press, Cambridge

Bangladesh Bureau of Statistics (BBS) (2010) 2009 statistical yearbook of Bangladesh. BBS, Dhaka

Bangladesh Bureau of Statistics (BBS) (2011) 2010 statistical yearbook of Bangladesh. BBS, Dhaka

Barkat A, Roy PK, Khan MS (2007) Charland in Bangladesh: political economy of ignored resources. Pathak Shamabesh, Dhaka

BRAC (2011) Annual report 2011, 40th year special edition. BRAC, Dhaka

Deaton A (1997) The analysis of household surveys: a microeconometric approach to development policy. Johns Hopkins University Press, Baltimore and London

Foster JE, Greer J, Thorbecke E (1984) A class of decomposable poverty measure. Econometrica 52(3):761–765

Grameen Bank (2011) Annual report 2011. Grameen Bank, Dhaka

Haughton J, Khandker SR (2009) Handbook on poverty and inequality. World Bank, Washington, DC

Khalily MAB, Latif MA (2010) Impact of prime intervention on monga mitigation in greater Rangpur region in Bangladesh. Institute of Microfinance, Dhaka

Khandker SR (1998) Fighting poverty with microcredit: experience in Bangladesh. Oxford University Press, New York

Khandker SR (2012) Seasonality of income and poverty in Bangladesh. J Dev Econ 97(2):244–256

Khandker SR, Mahmud W (2012) Seasonal hunger and public policies: evidence from Northwest Bangladesh. World Bank, Washington, DC

Khandker SR, Khalily MAB, Samad HA (2010) Seasonal and extreme poverty in Bangladesh: evaluating an ultra-poor microcredit project. Policy research working paper no. 5331. World Bank, Washington, DC

Lovell CH (1992) Breaking the cycle of poverty: the BRAC strategy. Kumarian Press, West Hartford, Connecticut

Morduch J (1999a) The microfinance promise. J Econ Lit 37(4):1569–1614

Morduch J (1999b) The role of subsidies in microfinance: evidence from the Grameen Bank. J Dev Econ 60(1):229–248

Palli Karma-Sahayak Foundation (PKSF) (2009) Annual progress report of PRIME & LIFT: FY 2008–2009. PKSF, Dhaka

Palli Karma-Sahayak Foundation (PKSF) (2011) Annual report 2011. PKSF, Dhaka

Rahman PMM, Matsui N, Ikemoto Y (2009) The chronically poor in rural Bangladesh: livelihood constraints and capabilities. Routledge, London and New York

Yunus M, Jolis A (1998) Banker to the poor: the autobiography of Muhammad Yunus, Founder of the Grameen Bank. University Press Limited, Dhaka

Chapter 4
Analysis of Socioeconomic Conditions and Seasonality in Northern Bangladesh: Based on Survey Data

Abu S. Shonchoy

Abstract This chapter addressed the findings derived from the baseline survey and short *monga* survey conducted in 2011 in northern Bangladesh. The surveys were intended to gather information for better understanding the socioeconomic conditions; state of *monga*; and problems faced by beneficiaries of the microcredit disbursed in collaboration with, a local NGO in northern Bangladesh.

Keywords Microcredit · Coping strategy · Socio-economic condition

4.1 Introduction

Focusing on the data set derived from the baseline survey conducted in July–August 2011 and the short lean period survey (hereafter, *monga* survey) conducted in October–November 2011, this chapter examines the socioeconomic conditions in northern Bangladesh, the depth of their severity, as well as the state of seasonality in the region. The data set is mainly derived from household-level questions, enabling us better comprehend individual and household-level characteristics as well as consumption and income irregularities during *monga*, people's various coping strategies, and the use of microcredit disbursed to 1,080 of the 1,440 households included in our study.

We conducted the baseline survey in mid-July 2011, after groups for microcredit were formed among the 72 randomly selected villages in Bangladesh's Kurigram and Rangpur districts. This survey consisted of several parts, designed to capture personal and household characteristics, income sources and occupational information, savings, debt and loan information, migration information, assets

A. S. Shonchoy (✉)
Institute of Developing Economies, Japan External Trade Organization,
3-2-2 Wakaba, Mihama-ku, Chiba-shi 261-8545, Japan
e-mail: parves.shonchoy@gmail.com

A. S. Shonchoy (ed.), *Seasonality and Microcredit*, SpringerBriefs in Economics,
DOI: 10.1007/978-4-431-55010-5_4,

(durable and non-durable), land information, and disaster information. To form the panel data set, in late October 2011, at the peak of *monga*, a short survey was conducted covering the same 1,440 households as the baseline survey. This survey had four sections on household-level scenarios, migration decisions, and credit use. In this chapter, we analyze the data derived from these baseline and short surveys.

4.2 Community-Level Data Analysis

At the beginning of our intervention, we asked our NGO counterpart Gana Unnayan Kendra (GUK), which has remarkable coverage in our study districts, to select villages on the basis of the following criteria:

- It receives no coverage from existing microfinance institutions (MFIs).
- It has been affected by *mongas* for the last 10 years (double-check with local administrative office).
- A majority of the families in the villages are ultra-poor.

On the basis of these selection criteria, GUK chose 92 villages: 57 from Gaibandha and 35 from Kurigram. Of these 92 villages, 26 were from *char* areas, 24 were classified as being in a river basin, and the remainder were classified as "inland." The geographical classification in the village selection was conducted mainly by GUK, as they considered these geographical groupings essential to our understanding of the proposed intervention's heterogeneous impact. As previously discussed, *char* is a local term for water-locked river islands in Bangladesh. We use the term "river basin" in reference to mainland areas around the Jamuna River and its tributaries that are vulnerable to flood and erosion-related disasters similar to those that afflict *char* areas. In terms of exposure to floods and erosions, river basin inhabitants are as vulnerable as *char* people. In terms of the infrastructure's ability to cope with flood and erosion risks, however, river basin inhabitants are less vulnerable because river basin areas are directly connected to inland areas by road, whereas *char* areas are isolated.

For our final village selection, we randomly chose 72 of the 92 villages. In the randomization process, we stratified villages on the basis of distance from a nearby bus station and village location type (i.e., *char*, river basin, or inland). Forty-four of the 72 villages (61.1 %) were from Gaibandha District, while the remainder (38.9 %) were from Kurigram District. Eighteen of the 72 villages (25.0 %) were from *char* areas, 42 (58.3 %) were from inland areas, and the rest (12; 16.7 %) were from river basin areas. These 72 villages are diverse in terms of available public facilities. For instance, if we compare Fig. 4.1a, b, which display public facilities by district and subdistrict, it appears that our sample villages from Kurigram are slightly better off in terms of education, transportation, and networking connectivity than those in Gaibandha. On the other hand, if we examine

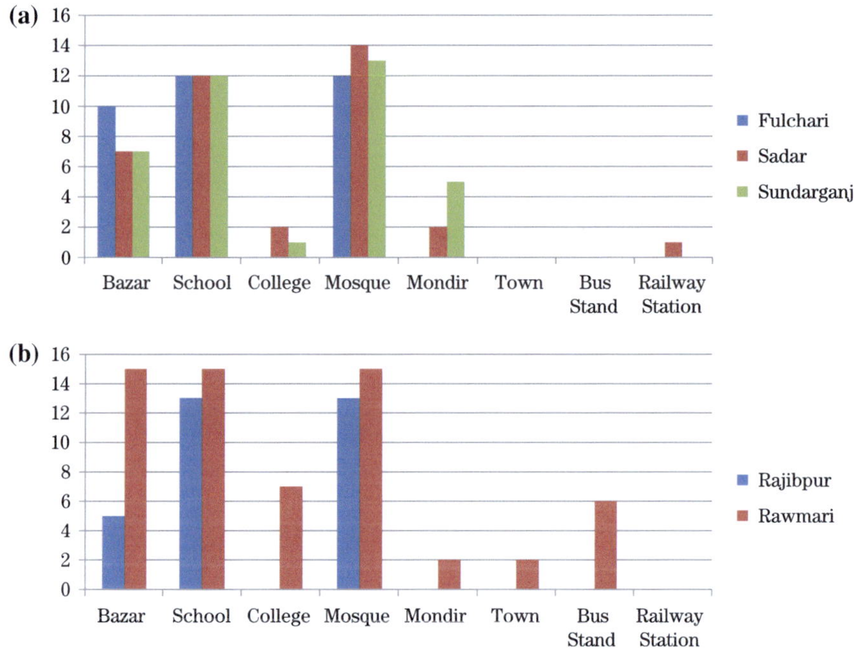

Fig. 4.1 Public facilities in sample villages in **a** Gaibandha district, **b** Kurigram district

the geographical categorization of public facilities among the sampled villages, the *char* areas emerge as the most deprived in terms of transportation and networking connectivity (Fig. 4.2).

4.3 Baseline Data Analysis

Following village selection, our counterpart NGO, GUK, formed a credit group locally known as *Shamity*, on the basis of their member-selection criteria, which were as follows:

- Must not own land amounting to more than 50 decimals[1];
- Possess productive assets worth no more than BDT 5,000;
- Must not own more than two goats/sheep, 10 fowl, or one shared cow;
- Must not be receiving cash/asset grants from another program; and
- Must have no regular source of income.

[1] 1 decimal = 1/100 acre or 40.46 m^2.

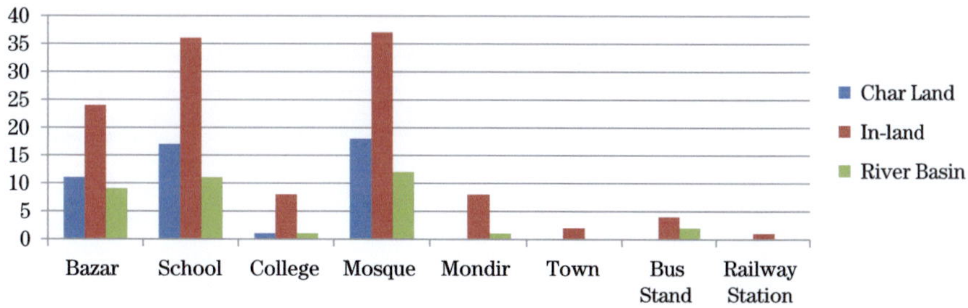

Fig. 4.2 Public facilities by geographical location

Fig. 4.3 Gender composition of household heads

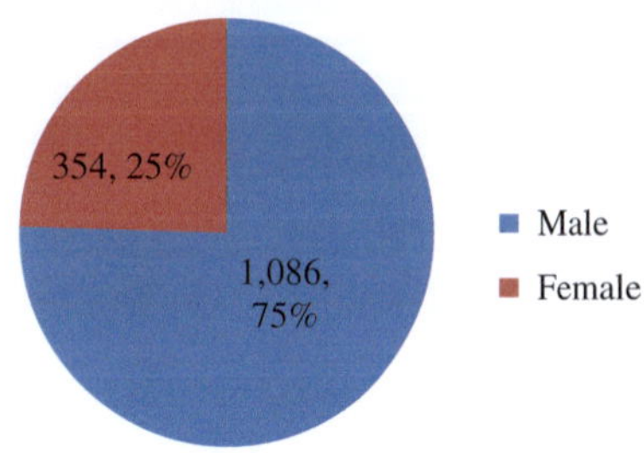

Following group formation, we conducted the baseline survey. As mentioned above, our baseline survey collected detailed information on individual and household-level characteristics. Consistent with national statistics, our sample found one-fourth of household heads to be female (see Fig. 4.3); the gender composition of household heads based on geographical classification also showed a similar trend (Fig. 4.4). However, in Fig. 4.5, we plot the gender composition of all observations across the 1,440 surveyed households; according to this, the distribution of the overall sample appears considerably more balanced.

In our sample, household heads had a mean age of 40.89 years, whereas for all observations within the full sample, it was 23.56 years. Across the various geographical locations, we found a similar pattern for mean estimated age, varying from 40.43 years (in inland areas) to 41.96 years (in *char* areas). In terms of gender-specific means, in our sample, we found the mean age of woman-headed households to be higher (44.25 years) than that of man-headed ones (39.79 years); for the full sample, the gender composition of age was similar (23.27 years and 23.84 years for the male and female subsamples, respectively). The distributions of age are depicted in Figs. 4.6 and 4.7.

In terms of the literacy rate, only 18 % of household heads could read and write, whereas a staggering 30 % are completely illiterate (Fig. 4.8). Literacy among household heads shows a sharp disparity between men and women: only 10 % of female household heads were educated—less than half the corresponding figure among their male counterparts (21 %). Literacy rates based on geographical classification do not dramatically differ, though we found women to be less educated in *char* areas than in inland areas (Fig. 4.9).

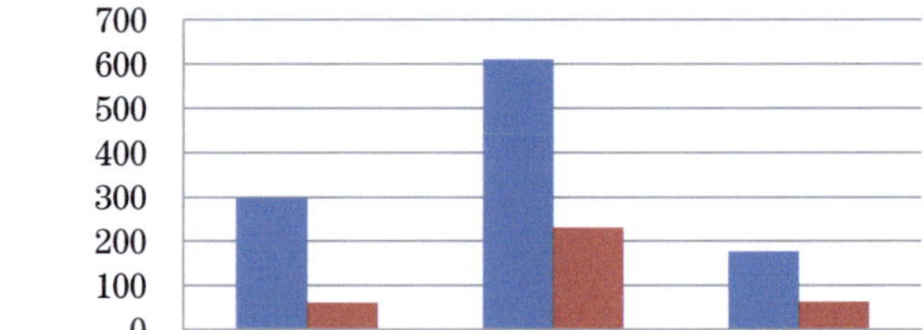

	Char Land	In-land	River Basin
Male	299	610	177
Female	61	230	63

Fig. 4.4 Geographical classification of household heads by gender

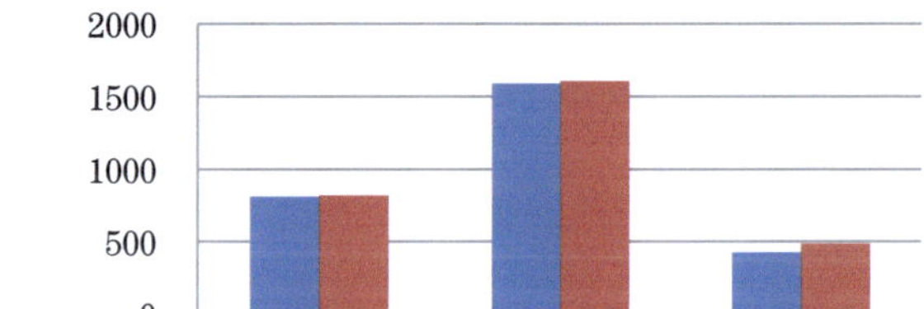

	Char Land	In-land	River Basin
Male	813	1,589	428
Female	820	1,605	485

Fig. 4.5 Gender composition of all household members by geographical classification

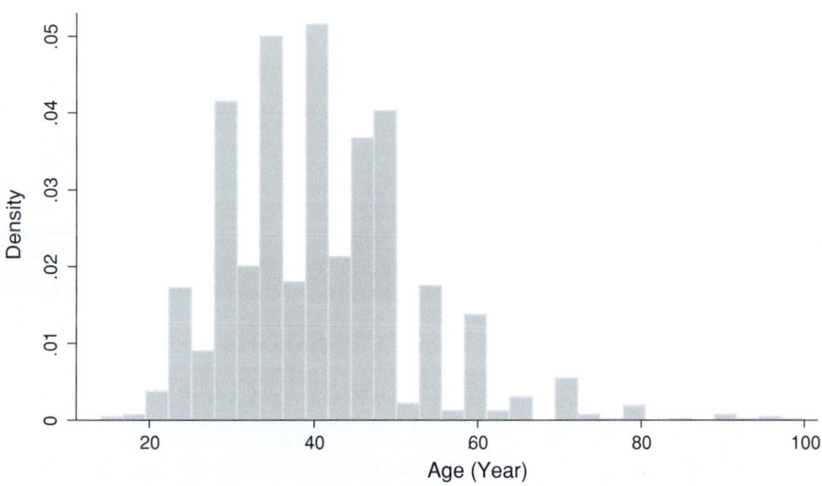

Fig. 4.6 Age distribution of household heads

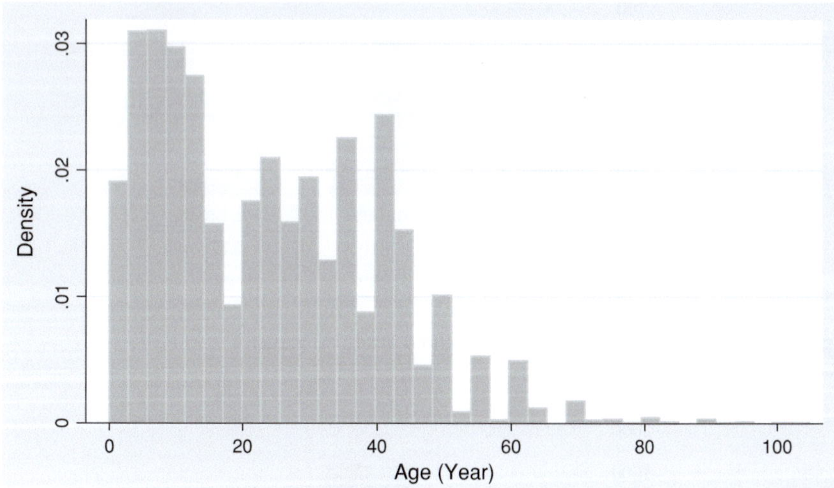

Fig. 4.7 Age distribution of full sample

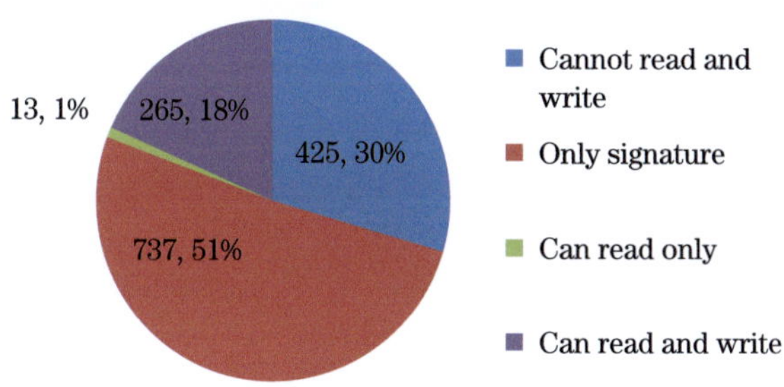

Fig. 4.8 Literacy rates among household heads

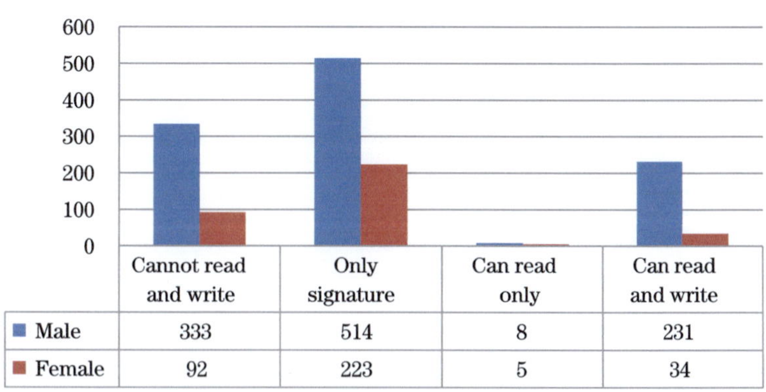

Fig. 4.9 Literacy rates among household heads by gender

Table 4.1 Household land holdings (in decimals)

	Agricultural	Pond	Homestead	Other
Mean	25.481	20.523	5.268	5.116
N	54	44	586	398
Summation	1,376.000	903.000	3,087.250	2,036.000
Standard Deviation	19.332	27.166	5.392	4.666

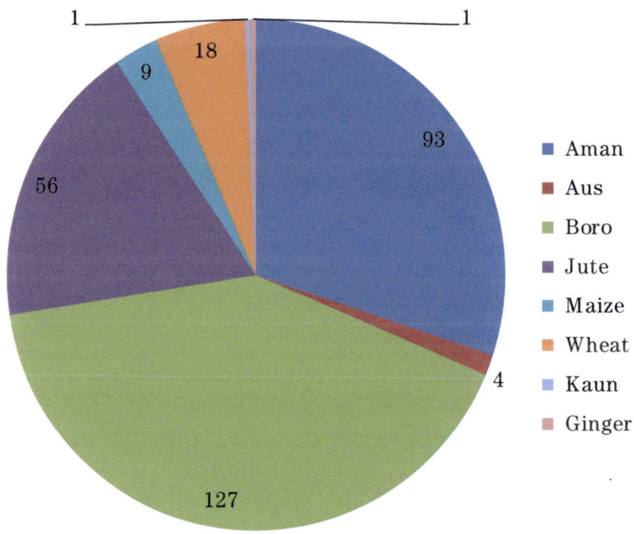

Fig. 4.10 Agricultural production among survey households

Other characteristics are also worth mentioning. In terms of religious affiliation, an overwhelming majority of our sample were Muslim (91.71 %), followed by Hindu (8.12 %). As for the household head's marital status, 83.82 % were married, 11.6 % were widowed, and 2.22 % were unmarried. In our sample, only 3.75 % possessed agricultural land, and the average land holding was about 25.48 decimals (Table 4.1). We gathered information on other forms of land holding from respondent households (e.g., ponds and homesteads), but these were mostly very small. Agricultural land was mainly used for rice production (Fig. 4.10), followed by jute, wheat, and maize. In terms of geographical differences in land use, we found that inland villages mostly produce rice. However, *char* land has been found to produce jute, wheat, and maize, which is not surprising as the soil and climate of *char* areas are more suitable for these crops (Table 4.2).

In northern Bangladesh, a large proportion of poor households are landless and asset-less. As a result, the majority is employed as agricultural wage labor, leaving them vulnerable to being affected by *mongas*. In our sample, about 84 % of household heads were wage laborers in either the agricultural or non-agricultural sectors. The breakdown presented in Fig. 4.11 shows that that more than half

Table 4.2 Agricultural production by geographical classification of households

Crop name	*Char*	Inland	River basin	Total
Aman (rice)	28	59	6	93
Aus (rice)	1	3	0	4
Boro (rice)	17	93	17	127
Jute	36	18	2	56
Maize	7	1	1	9
Wheat	13	5	0	18
Kaun	1	0	0	1
Ginger	0	1	0	1

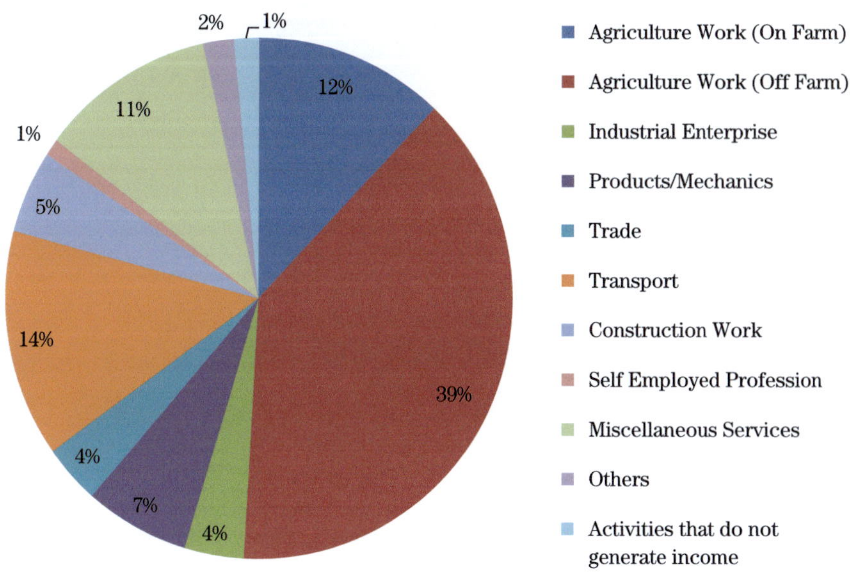

Fig. 4.11 Occupational distribution of household heads

(51 %) of these wage laborers were involved in seasonal work, meaning that they had no regular source of income and were bound to be affected by seasonality in the agricultural sector. They worked mostly within the same village (55 %) or in another village within the same union (24 %). Only a small proportion (6 %) of sample households had active wage employment in other districts (see Fig. 4.12). In our observed sample, about 14 % of household heads were not native to their residential locations. As shown in Fig. 4.13, river erosion was the main driver of migration to their current village; this is indicative of the degree of vulnerability these people face.

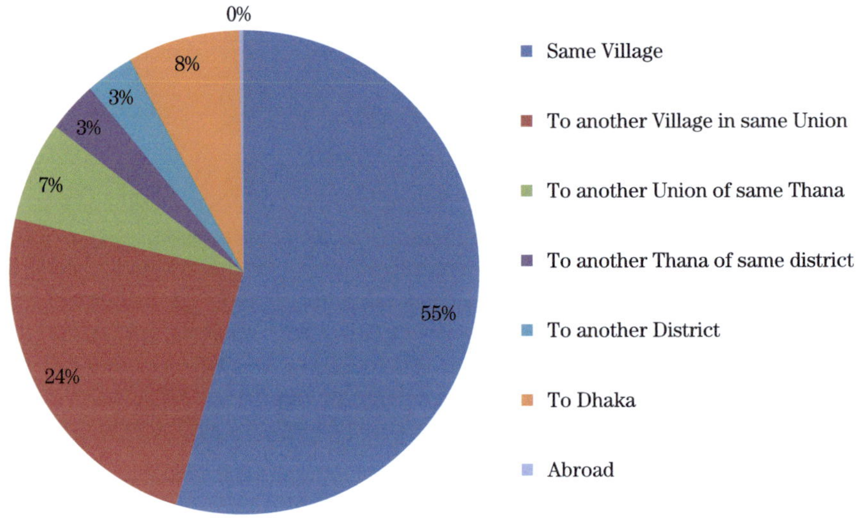

Fig. 4.12 Work location choices of household heads

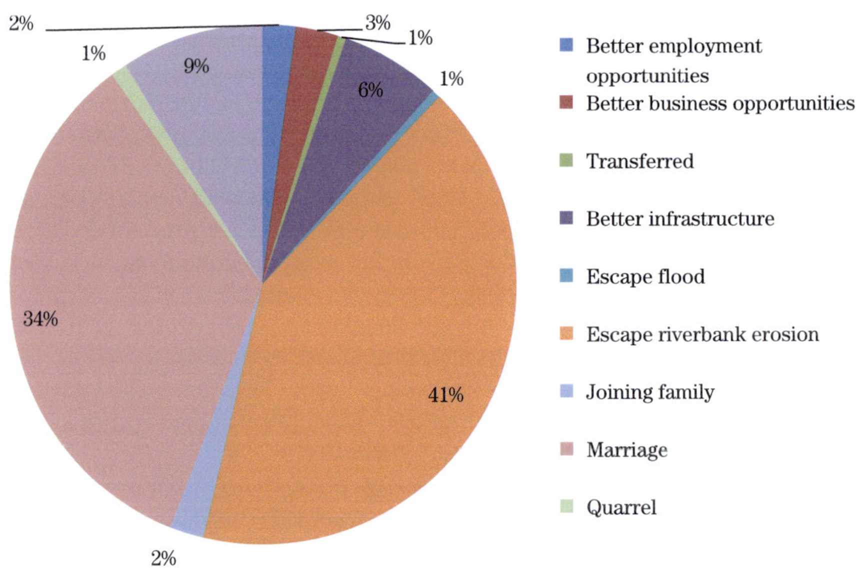

Fig. 4.13 Reason for inward migration by household heads

4.4 *Monga* Survey Data Analysis

4.4.1 Household-Level Scenario

The recent influential study by Khandker (2012) analyzes the nationally representative Household Income and Expenditure Surveys (HIES) of 2000 and 2005 and emphasizes the lower food consumption among households that suffer from seasonality, in spite of the decline in food prices in the region during *monga*. Seasonality-driven temporary unemployment during *monga* is the main reason for this reduced food consumption. One could argue that seasonal food shortages could be another reason for this phenomenon; however, both rounds of HIES confirmed that overall food-grain prices in both the northern districts and the rest of Bangladesh fall during the *monga* season, indicating that the "temporary food shortage" story is not plausible.

We examine Fig. 4.14, which includes unemployment (if the chief household income earner is jobless at the time of the survey), food crises (if the number of stomach-full meals per day is lower than average), and government assistance (if the household received support from the government under a social safety net designed to mitigate *mongas*). From Fig. 4.14, a bar diagram that shows the geographical classifications of our sample villages, it is clear that people living in Gaibandha District experience sharply restricted food consumption. Our study also revealed that on average, 31 % of our sample did not have any employment at the time of the survey. The last bar in Fig. 4.14 shows that the typical safety net provided by the government to mitigate *mongas* was overwhelmingly inadequate as well as ineffective. Only about 23 % of our sample received support under the Vulnerable Group Development program, a special safety net program dedicated to tackling food consumption reductions during *monga*. Furthermore, it is clear from Fig. 4.14 that river basin villages are more vulnerable than the other two types of village, primarily due to periodic flooding and river erosion. Oddly, the percentage of safety-net program beneficiaries during *monga* was lowest in river basin villages compared with the other village types. This indicates large-scale targeting failure by government organizations when implementing effective safety-net programs to deal with the impacts of seasonality.

There is no alternative agricultural activity in the lean season, and the non-agricultural sector cannot sufficiently absorb seasonally unemployed labor following plantation of the *Aman* crop. Figure 4.15 shows that even in the middle of the acute *monga* period, about 14 % of people had no job and more than half the sample had fewer than four days of paid work.

To compare food consumption during *monga* with that during the non-*monga* period, we asked detailed questions regarding the number of stomach-full meals as well as regarding egg, meat, fish, and milk consumption during both *monga* and non-*monga* periods. Table 4.3 contains summary statistics with respect to the respondents' replies. Particularly striking is the finding that some households consumed only one meal per day during the lean season; caloric intake during

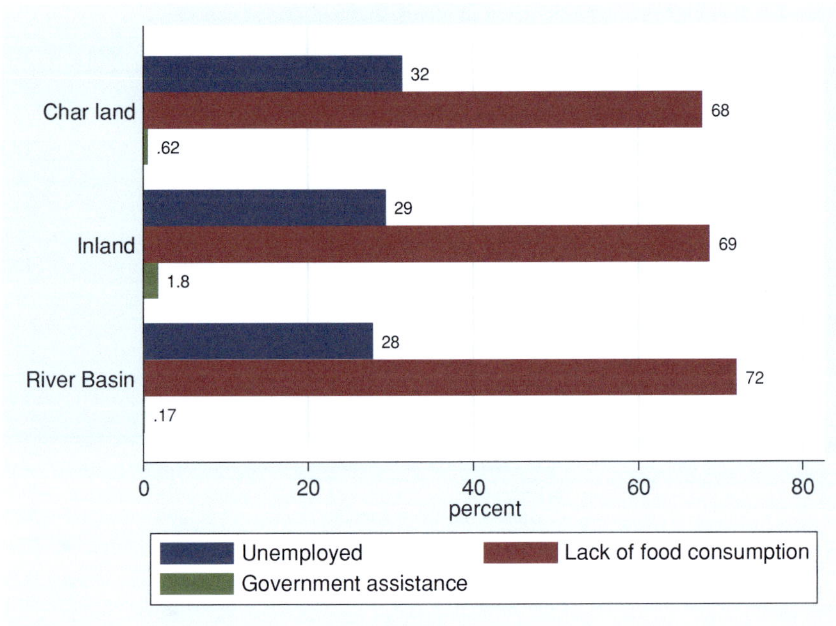

Fig. 4.14 *Monga* situation in Gaibandha

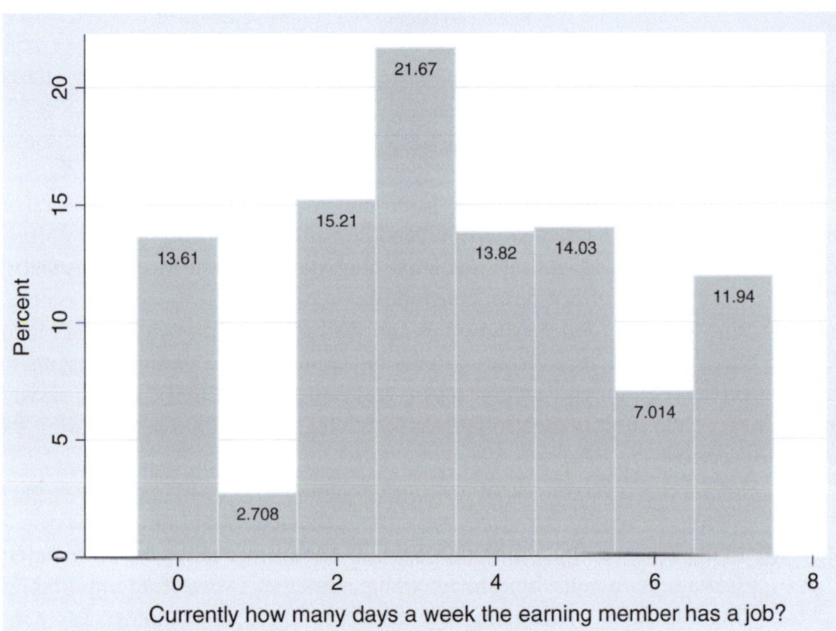

Fig. 4.15 *Monga* situation in 2011 for earning household members

Table 4.3 Household food consumption in *Monga* and non-*monga* periods

	Mean	SD	Min	Max
Normal: How many meals do you have in a day?	2.36	0.48	1	4
Monga: How many meals do you have in a day?	1.62	0.55	1	3
Normal: How many eggs do you have in a week?	1.65	2.16	0	18
Monga: How many eggs do you have in a week?	0.45	1.31	0	16
Normal: How frequently you have meat in a month?	0.04	0.27	0	4
Monga: How frequently you have meat in a month?	0.02	0.15	0	2
Normal: How frequently you have fish in a month?	2.34	1.51	0	12
Monga: How frequently you have fish in a month?	1.14	1.17	0	12
Normal: How frequently you have milk in a week?	0.18	0.75	0	7
Monga: How frequently you have milk in a week?	0.07	0.58	0	7

Table 4.4 Household coping strategies during *monga* periods

Coping strategy	Nos.	(%)
1. Savings	382	26.53
2. Borrowing from friends	299	20.76
3. Borrowing from landlords	247	17.15
4. Buying goods on credit	165	11.46
5. Migration	26	1.81
6. Advance sale of labor	12	0.83
7. Finding alternative work	58	4.03
8. MFI loans	7	0.49
9. Selling household assets	9	0.63
10. Selling livestock	12	0.83
11. No response	223	15.49
Total	1,440	100.00

Source Compiled by the author using data from a short *monga* survey conducted in November 2011

monga was significant lower than the minimum average required for an active, functional life. Detailed information on food consumption during *monga* corroborates this conclusion and outlines the same facts with respect to the seasonality suffered by the people of northern Bangladesh.

Drastically lowered food consumption can lead to problems with metabolism, the digestive system, undernutrition (including deficiencies in micronutrients as well as macronutrients), and weight loss (Ivers and Cullen 2009). In our survey, almost 16 % of the respondents self-reported having suffered a disease during the seasonality period.

Since *monga* is a seasonal phenomenon, one could expect households to have effective coping strategies to deal with the expected temporary joblessness, especially in the absence of an appropriate credit market and adequate government support. Information on household-level coping strategies is therefore important to understanding the level of vulnerability faced by these households. Table 4.4 shows the distribution of coping strategies among the surveyed households. It is worth noting that less than 1 % (0.5 %) of respondents considered borrowing from

Table 4.5 Household-level data on use of microcredit offered by GUK

	Nos.	(%)
1. Investment in nonagricultural business	305	28.24
2. Investment in livestock, including poultry	282	26.11
3. Consumption, including houses, ceremonies, and medical costs	139	12.87
4. Payment for debt and interest	69	6.39
5. Others (not specified)	61	5.65
6. Investment in farming	60	5.56
7. Investment in household productive assets	56	5.19
8. Transfer to the husband	45	4.17
9. No response	63	5.83
Total	1,080	100.0

Source Compiled by the author using data from a short *monga* survey executed in November 2011

MFIs as a coping strategy, even though such microfinance borrowing enables the poor to engage in non-agricultural activities and thus mitigate seasonality-induced suffering. Such findings may not be surprising given that microcredit offered by MFIs mostly have inflexible contracts, high interest rates, and strict loan repayment rules (e.g., a weekly payment that starts one week after loan disbursement and obligatory weekly meetings). In situations such as reductions in income due to a lean period that is extended but known to be finite, uncertain incomes plus the requirement for immediate repayment means MFIs' strict weekly repayment rules could adversely affect the poor by further reducing their food consumption and pushing them deeper into debt.

4.4.2 Credit Scenario

In the credit section of the survey questionnaire, we asked beneficiaries about the use of credit provided to them through GUK, our counterpart NGO in northern Bangladesh. We were particularly interested in knowing the beneficiaries' main purpose of accessing the loan, their current activities involving the credit, and their repayment plans.

The data set (Table 4.5) indicates that a large majority of beneficiaries invested the credit amount, either in their existing business (28.24 %) or in livestock (26.11 %). However, some spent their credit amount on non-productive activities such as paying outstanding debts (6.39 %) and household consumption (12.87 %).

Interestingly, more than 50 % of the beneficiaries planned to repay the credit installments from their regular job earnings (either their own or those of another family member), not from earnings derived from the business in which they had invested the credit amount. We also asked respondents whether they expected to earn larger incomes as a result of receiving the credit. Surprisingly, about 32 %

chose “do not know” as their answer. Of those who answered positively, 20.09 % were planning to spend the extra income from the business on family expenses, while 20.28 % were planning to buy assets for their respective households. Most recipients reported that their average number of working hours increased after receiving the credit.

The final question in the survey’s credit section asked respondents about their preferences regarding repayment schedules. Interestingly, 41.20 % of them did not suggest an alternate preferred method, while 25.09 % suggested a monthly installment scheme.

4.5 Conclusion

This chapter addressed the findings derived from the baseline survey and short *monga* survey conducted in 2011 in northern Bangladesh. The surveys were intended to gather information for better understanding the socioeconomic conditions; state of *monga*; and problems faced by beneficiaries of the microcredit disbursed in collaboration with GUK, a local NGO with two decades of experience with social issues in northern Bangladesh.

In addition, this chapter discussed the sampled villages, the geographical features of the surveyed area, and the survey questionnaires themselves. We also described key findings of various survey subsections that could be classified as capturing individual and household-level characteristics as well as geographical information. Largely employing descriptive statistics and a diagrammatic approach, this chapter drew particular attention to the phenomenon of *mongas*, which occur regularly among the poor and vulnerable people of northern Bangladesh.

References

Ivers LC, Cullen KA (2009) HIV/AIDS, Undernutrition, and food insecurity. Clin Infect Dis 49(7):1096–1102

Khandker SR (2012) Seasonality of income and poverty in Bangladesh. J Dev Econ 97(2):244–256

Chapter 5
Experimental Design for Flexible Microcredit Trials

Takashi Kurosaki

Abstract This chapter explains the experimental design of the randomized controlled trials we conducted in northern Bangladesh to examine the impact of seasonality-adjusted flexible microcredit, targeting the ultra-poor. In addition to describing our experimental design, this chapter compares the means of the characteristics of sample villages and households across various treatment arms. It reveals that most observable characteristics prior to our intervention were very similar across treatment arms, indicating that randomization was properly implemented. Descriptive analysis of the baseline survey data also indicates that our sample households belong to the poorest section of the rural Bangladesh.

Keywords Microcredit · Randomized controlled trial · Seasonality · Bangladesh

5.1 Introduction

This chapter describes the experimental design employed to evaluate the impact of flexible microfinance interventions. It also characterizes the sample households using survey data. As shown in Chaps. 2 and 3, the success of microcredit in poverty reduction has an important limitation: it is typically not offered to the poorest of the poor (often called the "ultra-poor"). Lending to the ultra-poor may be too risky for microfinance institutions (MFIs), even when using group-lending designs. At the same time, the ultra-poor may refrain from borrowing because of a fear of accumulating debt and uncertainty over their ability to meet the regular repayments demanded by a typical Grameen-style microcredit scheme.

T. Kurosaki (✉)
Hitotsubashi University, 2-1 Naka, Kunitachi, Tokyo 186-8603, Japan
e-mail: kurosaki@ier.hit-u.ac.jp

A. S. Shonchoy (ed.), *Seasonality and Microcredit*, SpringerBriefs in Economics,
DOI: 10.1007/978-4-431-55010-5_5,

In an attempt to enhance the ultra-poor's welfare level, this study examines what would happen if a typical Grameen-style microcredit scheme were "relaxed" in terms of repayment scheduling. As shown in Chap. 3 and the existing literature (Shonchoy 2011; Khandker 2012), seasonal deprivation associated with *monga* is a serious threat that affects the Bangladeshi poor in general and the ultra-poor of northern Bangladesh in particular. *Monga* refers to the period from September to November, after the transplanting but before the harvest of *Aman* paddy, the main rice variety in Bangladesh. During this period, farmers face seasonal unemployment coupled with rising commodity prices (especially the price of rice), which limit their purchasing power (Khandker 2012). Suffering related to *monga* can intensify when monsoon flooding is more intense than usual. In this context, provision of microcredit to the ultra-poor could enhance their welfare if repayment schedules can accommodate borrowers' special needs during *monga*.

Despite the potential for slightly altered microcredit arrangements to substantially reduce seasonal deprivation, the existing literature lacks rigorous evaluation of the impact of such flexibility in microcredit design. Among the few existing studies, Shoji (2010) evaluates the effectiveness of Bangladeshi microfinance following the introduction of a contingent repayment system beginning in 2002. This system allowed affected members to reschedule savings and installments during times of natural disaster. Using evidence pertaining to flooding in 2004 and using an instrumental variable approach, Shoji finds that rescheduling served as a safety net by substantially decreasing the probability of borrowers skipping meals in response to negative shocks; the effect was even more pronounced on the landless and women. Furthermore, if we restrict our attention to studies in the context of *monga*-related seasonal deprivation in northern Bangladesh, we find a similar dearth of qualitative research. Khandker and Mahmud (2012) use non-experimental data to analyze the correlates of seasonal deprivation while focusing on social protection programs and microcredit. Czura et al. (2011) examine the impact of repayment flexibility by conducting a randomized experiment with Indian dairy farmers. They show that repayment flexibility contributed to consumption smoothing and enhanced demand for credit. With the exception of Czura et al. (2011), we are unaware of any rigorous study based on a randomized controlled trial (RCT) design that examines the impact of repayment flexibility in South Asia.

Therefore, we initiated RCT experiments in northern Bangladesh in early 2011. In this chapter, we explain our experimental design and purpose. We used the RCT approach to investigate the impact of repayment flexibility in mitigating seasonality-induced deprivation in northern Bangladesh. The experiments were conducted in partnership with an NGO called Gana Unnayan Kendra (GUK). GUK is based in the Gaibandha District of northern Bangladesh, where the ultra-poor population is concentrated owing to severe *monga* and frequent flooding from the Jamuna River.

The chapter is organized as follows. Section 5.2 describes our RCT design. Section 5.3 explains the field implementation of our surveys and RCT interventions. More detailed discussions regarding GUK and its past activities are also provided. Using the baseline survey data, Sect. 5.4 shows that our RCT was successfully implemented with regard to guaranteeing exogenous variation in microcredit repayment designs. Section 5.5 summarizes the chapter.

5.2 RCT Strategy

5.2.1 Inflexible Microcredit as the Control

A typical Grameen-style microcredit scheme proceeds as follows (Armendariz and Morduch 2010). Persons eligible for microcredit first form a group wherein members are expected to help each other in times of difficulty.[1] Not all members can borrow immediately. Usually, only some are offered credit after all members have regularly saved a small amount of money; the rest are given credit after the first borrowers successfully repay several installments and all members continue to save the same small amount on a regular basis. Weekly repayments begin without a long grace period. With typical Grameen-type microcredit, the amount first lent is small and is to be repaid in 50 weekly installments within a 12-month period.

Several rationales have been offered for this rigidly designed repayment schedule (Armendariz and Morduch 2010). The success of frequent repayment in minimizing defaults and delays can be attributed to its function as an early warning mechanism, the lender's capture of information vis-à-vis the borrower's income flow, and the borrower's commitment to save regularly. Repayment in group meetings in front of others also motivates regular repayment by borrowers desiring to maintain their reputation within the village.

These mechanisms are likely responsible for classic Grameen-type microcredit's success in maintaining high repayment rates.[2] However, the requirement to attend regular weekly meetings places a high burden on the borrowers in terms of the opportunity costs of their time (Field et al. 2012). Borrowers therefore request the relaxation of several classic Grameen-type features. Academic research has responded to this request by seeking to identify the key element in guaranteeing high repayment rates. For example, using a field experiment approach, Giné and Karlan (2011) evaluate the impact of removing group liability in the Philippines; they find no adverse impact on repayments as long as public and frequent repayment systems were maintained. On the other hand, recent RCT design-based studies comparing weekly and monthly installments show mixed results. In India, Field and Pande (2008) show no differences between

[1] It is debatable whether this occurs only in terms of moral support or also implies joint liability in a legally enforceable sense; nonetheless, this debate is irrelevant to our context.

[2] See Kurosaki and Khan (2012) for an exceptional case in which an MFI suffered from high default rates despite adopting a Grameen-type credit scheme. In this case, weak enforcement of the contingent renewal rule led strategic default to prevail among borrowers.

microfinance schemes with weekly and monthly repayment frequencies as long as repayments were made in public meetings. The same RCT also shows that a change from weekly to monthly repayment greatly reduced borrowers' financial stress (Field et al. 2012). On the other hand, in Indonesia, Feigenberg et al. (2011) find that repayment performance was better when repayments were collected weekly rather than monthly.

Given this background, we adopted the following borrowing and repayment scheme as the control. Borrowers obtain BDT 3,000[3] of credit and begin repayment after a 2-week grace period. Repayments are made in 45 installments of BDT 75 each (except for the last payment, which is BDT 60), implying a gross interest payment of BDT 360 spread throughout the borrowing period of approximately 1 year. Each weekly installment is to be repaid by the borrower at a weekly meeting, which the borrower is obliged to attend, even during *monga*. This is the typical design of a traditional or inflexible microcredit scheme, which we denote as the "Control."

5.2.2 Flexible Microcredit as the Treatment

During the agriculturally lean *monga* period, microcredit borrowers may face difficulties in acquiring the money for regular repayment. To facilitate the demand for repayment flexibility in this context, the treatment relaxes the repayment schedule in one of two ways during the *monga* period, which for this purpose is designated as September 20–December 20.

Under the first treatment arm, "Flexible 1," a temporary repayment moratorium is granted during the designated *monga* period. During the moratorium, Flexible 1 households do not pay any installments. After *monga*, borrowers pay BDT 100 per week, ensuring that their total repayment amount and repayment period are identical to those in the Control.

One-third of the participants randomized to receive Flexible 1 treatment are also given income-generation activities (IGA) support. We refer to this treatment arm as "Flexible 1 + IGA." With IGA support, instead of providing cash, we provide microcredit borrowers with a productive asset of their choice within the credit amount as well as advice for utilizing the asset; no further subsidy is provided.

Under the second flexibility treatment arm, "Flexible 2," the repayment schedule is changed to feature three monthly installments of BDT 300 each during the designated *monga* period, instead of 12 weekly repayments of BDT 75 each. After *monga*, borrowers resume paying BDT 75 per week; thus, their total repayment amount and repayment period are the same as those of the Control.

---

[3] BDT 100 is equivalent to approximately JPY 99 or USD 1.22. BDT 3,000 therefore equals approximately USD 37.

5.2.3 Randomization of Treatment Arms

To preclude unequal treatment among members within a group, we randomized the four treatment arms at the borrower-group level. Since our counterpart NGO usually forms one group per village, our randomization took place at the village level.

Of the 90 villages under potential treatment by the counterpart NGO, we randomly selected 12 villages for "Control," 24 for "Flexible 1," 12 for "Flexible 1 + IGA," and 24 for "Flexible 2." In the randomization, we stratified the villages on the basis of their distance from the closest bus station and their location type (see Sect. 5.3.1).

More villages were randomized to "Flexible 1" and "Flexible 2" than to "Flexible 1 + IGA" and "Control" because our initial design had another experimental dimension, distinguished by the timing when borrower groups would be informed about the relaxation of their repayment schedule. The intention was to create exogenous variation in the information structure, as implemented by Karlan and Zinman (2009) in the context of consumer credit in South Africa. However, due to delays in group formation and loan disbursement, the exact timing of the announcement was similar across all groups. Therefore, in analyzing the impact of our experiment, we eventually merged these two types of treatments (initially designated as "surprise" and "pre-announced flexibility").

In each village, GUK formed a borrower group known as a *samity*, comprising 20 members who satisfied the NGO's microcredit criteria and expressed interest in receiving microcredit. Member names were then recorded in the *samity*-formation book by the loan officers. In the book, each member was assigned a number in ascending order; members who happened to hold numbers 1–15 were offered credit, while those holding numbers 16–20 were kept as observers. Initially we asked our NGO counterpart to include everyone in the borrowing group, however, after the group was formed and load disbursement was due, our counterpart NGO faced difficulty to finance everyone in the group and decided to finance only 15 out of 20 for each group. As a result, we told them to finance based on the shamity-formation book record and finance only the first 15 of that record book. This randomization design was not known to the *samity* members before the treatments were announced. The randomization thus implies the following sample distribution: 72 sample villages and 1,440 sample households, one-sixth or one-third of which fall into one of the four treatment arms; three-fourths of sample households (1,080 households) were actual borrowers of microcredit.

5.2.4 Empirical Strategy to Identify the Impact of Treatment

Let Y_{hj} be the post-intervention value of a welfare indicator for household h that received treatment arm j. We need to estimate $\mathrm{E}[Y_{hj}] - \mathrm{E}[Y_{hk}]$ to evaluate the impact of treatment j relative to treatment k; treatment k may be the Control or a different type of treatment. By definition, however, for each h, we can observe only one treatment status; therefore, this estimate was not readily available.

Nevertheless, if randomization is properly implemented, heterogeneity across households would become orthogonal to the treatment status. Under this condition, the simple test of difference in means between treatment arms j and k sufficiently shows the impact of j relative to that of k. In other words, we can use $\text{Avg}[Y_j] - \text{Avg}[Y_k]$ as an unbiased estimate for $\text{E}[Y_{hj}] - \text{E}[Y_{hk}]$. In Sect. 5.4, we provide empirical results regarding whether our randomization resulted in groups that are similar *ex ante* across treatment arms.

A comparison of the post-intervention endogenous variable between the Control and each of the other three treatment arms shows whether flexibility had an impact in comparison with the inflexible design. If some or all of the three treatment arms are associated with a statistically significant difference from the Control, we can compare two of the three treatment types and test the significance of the difference. To be more precise, let $k = 0$ (Control), and $j = 1$ (Flexible 1), 2 (Flexible 1 + IGA), or 3 (Flexible 2). If $\text{Avg}[Y_j] - \text{Avg}[Y_0]$ does not significantly differ from 0 for all $j = 1, 2, 3$, then flexibility has no impact; otherwise, flexibility has an impact. In such a case, the magnitude of $\text{Avg}[Y_2] - \text{Avg}[Y_1]$ indicates the additional impact that IGA support bestows. The magnitude of $\text{Avg}[Y_3] - \text{Avg}[Y_1]$ reflects which flexible treatment arm (temporary moratorium versus monthly rescheduling) has a larger impact.

5.3 Implementation of Surveys and RCT Interventions

5.3.1 Counterpart NGO and Study Area

GUK operates in the greater Gaibandha area, comprising five districts in northern Bangladesh: Gaibandha, Kurigram, Rangpur, Lalmonirhat, and Nilphamari. It has offices in all 32 *upazilas* (subdistricts) in Gaibandha District and five offices in the Kurigram District.

As explained in Chap. 4, distinguishing *char*, river basin, and inland areas is important in areas where our target group—the poor and vulnerable—live. Therefore, our randomization stratified villages on the basis of distance from the closest bus station and village location type (*char*, river basin, or inland). The distribution of our final sample villages is shown in Table 5.1. Forty-five of the 72 sample villages (62.5 %) were in Gaibandha District, and the remainder (37.5 %) were in Kurigram District. Eighteen of the 72 sample villages (25.0 %) were in *char* areas, 42 (58.3 %) were in inland areas, and the remaining 12 (16.7 %) were in river basin areas.

Table 5.1 Distribution of sample villages by treatment type, northern Bangladesh, 2011

	Treatment type				Grand total
	Flexible 1	Flexible 1 + IGA	Flexible 2	Control	
Total	24	12	24	12	72
By district and Upazila					
Gaibandha district	16	8	12	9	45
Fulchari	4	1	2	4	11
Gaibandha Sadar	6	7	7	1	21
Sundarganj	6	0	3	4	13
Kurigram district	8	4	12	3	27
Rajibpur	3	2	6	1	12
Rawmari	5	2	6	2	15
By location type					
Char	6	3	6	3	18
Inland	14	7	14	7	42
River Basin	4	2	4	2	12

Source Compiled by the author using data gathered through the baseline survey

5.3.2 Schedule of Household Surveys and Field Experiments

Figure 5.1 shows the timeline of our surveys and experiments. In the first half of 2011, we visited Gaibandha and GUK to undertake preparatory investigations and make logistical arrangements. Following our agreement with GUK regarding the research design, village-level randomization was implemented, followed by *samity* formation. The baseline survey (Panel 1) of 1,440 households, conducted in July–September 2011, captured detailed information on aspects such as the household roster; education; health, including children's weights; occupation; assets; income; migration experiences; agricultural production; non-agricultural enterprises; savings; credit; debt; and *monga* coping strategies.

In the first 3 weeks of September 2011, microcredit of BDT 3,000 each was issued to three-fourths of our sample households. Our initial plan was to issue the microcredit earlier. However, due to financing problem faced by GUK, owing to the holy month of Ramadan and the subsequent festival of Eid ul Fitr, disbursement was delayed. As a result, households given flexible microcredit entered the designated *monga* period before their first repayment installment's due date. Nevertheless, GUK was able to collect monthly installments (Flexible 2) and larger weekly installments in the post-*monga* period (Flexible 1) without experiencing serious delays or non-repayment problems (see Chap. 6). As designed, in all villages, 15 *samity* members were issued credit (i.e., three-fourths of the *samity* members).

After the RCT experiments began, and as of the time of writing, two additional surveys had been conducted: the first *monga* survey (Panel 2) in November 2011 and the follow-up survey (Panel 3) in July–August 2012. Panel 1 (the baseline survey) and Panel 3 were based on the long questionnaire, which covered all aspects of the household economy. On the other hand, Panel 2 was based on the

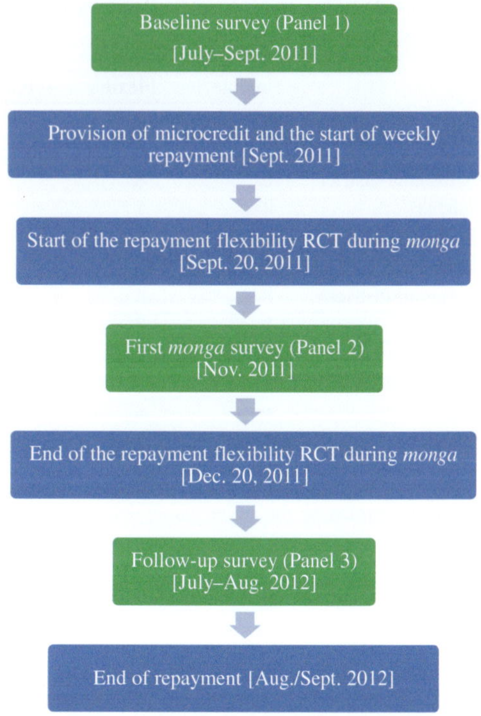

Fig. 5.1 Timeline of interventions and surveys. *Source* Prepared by the author. The *blue panels* show events regarding interventions, and the *green panels* show events regarding surveys

short questionnaire, which focused on how the household coped with ongoing *monga* difficulties. Panel 1 was intended to capture the state of affairs *before* our interventions, Panel 2 to describe the household economy *during* our interventions, and Panel 3 to collect information *after* our RCT experiments. In Panels 1 and 2, 1,440 households were surveyed. In Panel 3, 1,422 of the initial 1,440 households were resurveyed, indicating an attrition rate of 1.25 %.

5.4 Randomization Validity

5.4.1 Village-Level Variables

As our randomization was properly implemented, we expected no systematic difference in pre-intervention characteristics at the village level across treatment arms. To test this, we estimated the following village-level regression model using the baseline survey data:

$$X_v = b_0 + b_1 D_{1v} + b_2 D_{2v} + b_3 D_{3v} + u_v, \tag{5.1}$$

Table 5.2 Balance test at the village level: location

	Dependent variable		
	Distance from the closest bus station (km)	Dummy for a *char* village	Dummy for an in-land village
Intercept	32.167***	0.250*	0.583***
	[9.695]	[0.129]	[0.146]
*D*1 (dummy for flexible 1)	12.458	0.000	0.000
	[12.431]	[0.158]	[0.179]
*D*2 (dummy for flexible 1 + IGA)	10.333	0.000	0.000
	[14.172]	[0.182]	[0.207]
*D*3 (dummy for flexible 2)	15.25	0.000	0.000
	[12.426]	[0.158]	[0.179]
R^2	0.020	0.000	0.000
F-stat. for zero slopes of all dummies	0.537	0.000	0.000

Note The number of observations is 72. Robust standard errors are shown in brackets. Significant at the 10 % (*), 5 % (**), and 1 % (***) levels
Source Estimated by the author using baseline survey data

where X_v is a pre-intervention variable for village v, D_{jv} is a dummy variable for treatment j ($j = 1, 2, 3$; i.e., Flexible 1, Flexible 1 + IGA, and Flexible 2, respectively), and u_v is a zero mean error term. If the null hypothesis that $b_1 = b_2 = b_3 = 0$ is not rejected, the balance test is passed.

Table 5.2 shows the results when the distance from the closest bus station to the village, the dummy for a *char* village, and the dummy for an inland village were used as X_v. In all three specifications, the null hypothesis was not rejected, even at the 20 % level. In addition, all individual coefficients for the three dummy variables were also insignificant.[4] As our village-level randomization employed these measures as strata, the results in Table 5.2 were as expected.

To examine balance across treatment arms, similar models were applied to the village-level public facilities analyzed in Chap. 4. As primary schools and mosques exist in most surveyed villages, we excluded them during the balance check. Table 5.3 shows the results for the remaining six variables (bazar, college, Hindu temple, distance to nearest town, bus stand,[5] and railway station). For all six cases, the null hypothesis that $b_1 = b_2 = b_3 = 0$ was not rejected at the 5 % level. In this sense, the balance test was passed, suggesting that our randomization strategy at the village level was properly implemented.

[4] For convenience, Table 5.2 and all following tables show the estimate for the intercept in the first row, which is readily interpreted as the estimate for the overall mean if all coefficients on the three (four) dummy variables are zero.

[5] The "bus stand" here refers to the availability of any bus stand in the village, while the "bus station" used in our randomization strata refers to the distance from the closest bus station at which medium- and long-distance bus services are available.

Table 5.3 Balance test at the village level: public facilities

	Dependent variable: minutes of travel to the nearest facility					
	Bazar	College	Mondir (Hindu temple)	Town	Bus stand	Railway station
Intercept	7.917**	27.083***	29.583***	34.167***	29.583***	61.667***
	[3.711]	[6.764]	[8.100]	[7.666]	[6.764]	[16.069]
*D*1 (dummy for flexible 1)	1.042	3.75	3.125	8.958	26.292	18.750
	[4.536]	[7.833]	[9.846]	[8.661]	[21.057]	[19.620]
*D*2 (dummy for flexible 1 + IGA)	5.417	13.333*	25.000*	25.833**	24.583*	25.417
	[5.382]	[7.904]	[13.530]	[11.848]	[12.809]	[22.523]
*D*3 (dummy for flexible 2)	–0.417	1.875	16.458*	13.333	10.417	26.458
	[4.495]	[8.071]	[8.869]	[8.463]	[8.054]	[20.090]
R^2	0.026	0.047	0.109	0.109	0.028	0.028
F-stat. for zero slopes of all dummies	0.556	1.731	2.556*	1.807	1.549	0.649

Note The number of observations is 72. Robust standard errors are shown in brackets. Significant at the 10 % (*), 5 % (**), and 1 % (***) levels. Dependent variables are measured in minutes if public transportation is used, and the value 0 is assigned when a facility exists in the village
Source Estimated by the author, using baseline survey data

Nevertheless, the null hypothesis was rejected at the 10 % level for the case of Hindu temples, and the individual coefficient on D_{2v} was significant at the 5 % level for the case of distance to the nearest town. As we randomized the treatment status, we assessed these results as having occurred by chance. As shown in Chap. 7, these non-random components do not affect our impact analysis; see the results of the robustness check, undertaken by controlling for these baseline village-level variables.

5.4.2 Household-Level Variables

As our randomization was properly implemented, we expected no systematic differences in pre-intervention characteristics at the household level across the four treatment arms.[6] To test this, we estimated the following household-level regression model using the baseline survey data:

$$X_h = b_0 + b_1 D_{1h} + b_2 D_{2h} + b_3 D_{3h} + b_4 D_{4h} + u_h, \qquad (5.2)$$

[6] A difference might occur at the household level across treatment arms, as treatments were randomized at the village level. For example, Czura et al. (2011) state that "Differences in client characteristics are due to the fact that randomization occurred at the group level and groups form according to socioeconomic characteristics" (10).

Table 5.4 Balance test at the household level: household head characteristics

	Dependent variable			
	Age	Dummy for female	Dummy for literacy	Years of schooling
Intercept	38.672***	0.228***	0.239***	1.589***
	[1.142]	[0.063]	[0.038]	[0.246]
*D*1 (dummy for flexible 1)	−0.536	−0.036	−0.017	−0.186
	[1.296]	[0.081]	[0.045]	[0.287]
*D*2 (dummy for flexible 1 + IGA)	−0.411	−0.117	0.006	−0.183
	[1.376]	[0.070]	[0.070]	[0.362]
*D*3 (dummy for flexible 2)	−0.467	−0.058	−0.028	−0.189
	[1.259]	[0.078]	[0.048]	[0.307]
*D*4 (dummy for non-borrower)	−0.583	−0.022	−0.039	−0.198
	[1.206]	[0.063]	[0.041]	[0.273]
R^2	0.000	0.007	0.001	0.000
F-stat. for zero slopes of all dummies	0.06	1.54	0.44	0.14
F-stat. for zero slopes of *D*1, *D*2, and *D*3	0.06	1.31	0.16	0.16

Note The number of observations is 1,440, except for years of schooling, for which two observations are missing. Robust standard errors clustered at the village level are shown in brackets. Significant at the 10 % (*), 5 % (**), and 1 % (***) levels
Source Estimated by the author using the microdata described in the text

where X_h is a pre-intervention variable for household h, D_{jh} ($j = 1, 2, 3$) is a dummy variable indicating that household h was provided with flexible microcredit under treatment arm j ($j = 1, 2, 3$; i.e., Flexible 1, Flexible 1 + IGA, and Flexible 2, respectively), D_{4h} is a dummy for non-borrower households, and u_h is a zero mean error term. If the null hypothesis that $b_1 = b_2 = b_3 = 0$ is not rejected, the balance test is passed. If no selection bias occurred in assigning borrower versus non-borrower households within each *samity*, we expect b_4 to be zero as well. Because the randomization was implemented at the village level and sample households were drawn using the village as the primary sampling unit, we tested the null hypotheses using robust standard errors for b clustered at the village level.

From the baseline survey data,[7] we compiled four variables characterizing the household head, six characterizing household members, five characterizing land holdings, and five characterizing liquid asset ownership. Equation (5.2) was applied to these variables, and the regression results are reported in Tables 5.4, 5.5, 5.6 and 5.7.

[7] To be more precise, owing to data entry problems, we used Panel 3 data for the household demography variables (age was adjusted by 1 year), supplemented by Panel 1 data for the 22 attrition households. For land and assets, we used Panel 1 data.

Table 5.5 Balance test at the household level: household member characteristics

	Dependent variable: minutes of travel to the nearest facility					
	Household size	Average age	Female ratio	Ratio of adults (age 15+)	Literacy rate of adult males	Literacy rate of adult females
Intercept	3.722***	26.367***	0.557***	0.702***	0.277***	0.229***
	[0.211]	[1.238]	[0.021]	[0.026]	[0.038]	[0.037]
*D*1 (dummy for flexible 1)	0.328	−1.302	−0.022	−0.045	0.009	−0.014
	[0.257]	[1.404]	[0.026]	[0.030]	[0.047]	[0.042]
*D*2 (dummy for flexible 1 + IGA)	0.433	−2.166	−0.031	−0.039	0.030	0.108*
	[0.280]	[1.489]	[0.023]	[0.030]	[0.057]	[0.056]
*D*3 (dummy for flexible 2)	0.431*	−2.144	−0.044*	−0.077**	0.007	0.050
	[0.247]	[1.326]	[0.024]	[0.029]	[0.048]	[0.046]
*D*4 (Dummy for non-borrower)	0.078	0.246	−0.011	−0.016	0.019	0.001
	[0.211]	[1.333]	[0.023]	[0.030]	[0.044]	[0.041]
R^2	0.012	0.013	0.005	0.015	0.000	0.010
F-stat. for zero slopes of all dummies	2.59**	3.63***	1.42	4.95***	0.11	2.24*
F-stat. for zero slopes of *D*1, *D*2, and *D*3	1.12	1.13	1.27	2.85**	0.10	2.86**
Number of observations	1,440	1,437	1,440	1,440	1,252	1,428

Note Robust standard errors clustered at the village level are shown in brackets. Significant at the 10 % (*), 5 % (**), and 1 % (***) levels
Source Estimated by the author, using baseline survey data

Regarding the characteristics of household heads (Table 5.4), the average age of those who received inflexible microcredit was 38.7 years, insignificantly different from that of those provided with flexible microcredit schemes or those not provided with any microcredit. About 23 % of the household heads provided with inflexible microcredit were female; the female household head ratios were slightly lower among households provided with flexible microcredit, but the difference was statistically insignificant. About 24 % of the household heads in the Control were literate, with 1.6 years of schooling on average. Again, these education characteristics were similar across treatment arms.

Table 5.5 shows the regression results regarding the characteristics of the household rosters. The average Control household size comprised 3.7 persons, and their average household member age was 26.4 years. The ratio of females among members belonging to Control households was 56 %, while Control group adult literacy rates were 28 % for males. For these four variables, the null hypothesis that $b_1 = b_2 = b_3 = 0$ was not rejected, even at the 20 % level, indicating that the balance test was passed. Two exceptions were the ratio of adults to household

Table 5.6 Balance test at the household level: land holdings

	Dependent variable				
	Dummy for owning the house land	Dummy for owning farm land	Size of operational farm land for Aus	Size of operational farm land for *Aman*	Size of operational farm land for Boro
Intercept	0.306***	0.056**	0.567**	2.167***	2.339***
	[0.093]	[0.022]	[0.276]	[0.737]	[0.792]
*D*1 (dummy for flexible 1)	0.150	−0.033	0.956	0.242	1.294
	[0.113]	[0.023]	[0.804]	[1.160]	[1.254]
*D*2 (dummy for flexible 1 + IGA)	0.072	−0.022	0.728	0.322	−1.022
	[0.129]	[0.029]	[0.728]	[1.518]	[1.036]
*D*3 (dummy for flexible 2)	0.125	−0.017	−0.147	−1.222	−0.861
	[0.121]	[0.029]	[0.318]	[0.834]	[0.917]
*D*4 (dummy for non-borrower)	0.083	−0.014	0.753	0.186	0.553
	[0.090]	[0.023]	[0.621]	[1.162]	[1.041]
R^2	0.009	0.003	0.004	0.004	0.008
F-stat. for zero slopes of all dummies	0.67	0.88	1.01	1.17	1.82
F-stat. for zero slopes of *D*1, *D*2, and *D*3	0.65	0.85	1.17	1.46	1.68

Note The land size is measured by decimal, which is 0.01 acre. The number of observations is 1,440. Robust standard errors clustered at the village level are shown in brackets. Significant at the 10 % (*), 5 % (**), and 1 % (***) levels
Source Estimated by the author, using the microdata described in the text

members and the literacy rate of adult females. The average ratio of adults in households treated with Flexible 2 was 8 % points lower than that in households treated with inflexible microcredit, and the difference was statistically significant at the 5 % level. Because of the significance of this variable, the null hypothesis that $b_1 = b_2 = b_3 = 0$ was rejected at the 5 % level for the adult ratio. In the case of the literacy rate of adult females, the point estimate shows that households treated with Flexible 1 + IGA had literacy rates that were 11 % points higher than those in traditional microcredit households, a difference statistically significant at the 10 % level. Regarding the null hypothesis that $b_1 = b_2 = b_3 = b_4 = 0$, it was rejected at the 5 % level for three variables: average household size, average age, and the ratio of adults.

Regarding land holdings characteristics (Table 5.6), 31 % of Control households owned the land on which their house was built, and only 6 % owned farm land. The average farm land cultivated in the first, second, and third cropping seasons by households provided with inflexible microcredit was 0.006, 0.022, and 0.023 acres, respectively. Again, the difference between households under various treatment arms and the Control households was statistically insignificant. The absolute levels of these figures reported in Table 5.6 indicate that our sample

Table 5.7 Balance test at the household level: liquid assets

	Dependent variable				
	Total value of household assets (BDT)	Dummy for owning livestock animals	Number of cows and bulls owned	Number of goats and sheep owned	Number of chickens and ducks owned
Intercept	2,827***	0.656***	0.378***	0.464***	2.961***
	[333]	[0.076]	[0.097]	[0.128]	[0.717]
*D*1 (dummy for flexible 1)	425	0.039	0.117	0.042	0.250
	[527]	[0.091]	[0.139]	[0.161]	[0.837]
*D*2 (dummy for flexible 1 + IGA)	613	−0.011	0.272	0.153	−0.561
	[473]	[0.093]	[0.230]	[0.182]	[0.838]
*D*3 (dummy for flexible 2)	411	−0.025	0.003	0.092	−0.192
	[395]	[0.090]	[0.121]	[0.158]	[0.812]
*D*4 (dummy for non-borrower)	381	−0.042	0.069	0.011	−0.689
	[319]	[0.077]	[0.110]	[0.135]	[0.676]
R^2	0.002	0.004	0.009	0.002	0.005
F-stat. for zero slopes of all dummies	0.50	1.19	0.61	0.43	1.81
F-stat. for zero slopes of *D*1, *D*2, and *D*3	0.60	0.31	0.76	0.28	0.61

Note The household assets in the first column include radios, TVs, bicycles, motorcycles, sewing machines, electrical appliances, and mobile phones. The number of observations is 1,440. Robust standard errors clustered at the village level are shown in brackets. Significant at the 10 % (*), 5 % (**), and 1 % (***) levels

Source Estimated by the author, using the microdata described in the text

belonged to the poorest section of rural Bangladesh. This is the population segment targeted by our counterpart NGO.

Table 5.7 summarizes information on liquid assets owned by sample households. The average value of household assets owned by Control households—such as electric appliances, transport equipment, and sewing machines—was BDT 2,800, slightly smaller than the amount of microcredit provided under our RCT. The difference between Control and other households was statistically insignificant. The null hypothesis that $b_1 = b_2 = b_3 = 0$ was not rejected, even at the 20 % level. In rural Bangladesh, livestock are important assets that can be liquidated in times of need. The table shows that 66 % of Control households owned livestock animals; however, their livestock holdings were minimal: 0.38 cattle, 0.46 goats, and 3.0 chickens each, on average. These levels were insignificantly different from those of households treated under different arms, or non-borrower households. Again, Table 5.7 shows that our sample households were poor, even by Bangladeshi standards.

In summary, of the 20 variables analyzed in Tables 5.4, 5.5, 5.6 and 5.7, only two cases (i.e., the ratio of adults in the household roster and the literacy rate of adult females) saw the null hypothesis that $b_1 = b_2 = b_3 = 0$ rejected at the 5 % level; only three cases (i.e., the household size, average age of members, and the ratio of adults) saw the null hypothesis that $b_1 = b_2 = b_3 = b_4 = 0$ rejected at the 5 % level. If we individually assess the significance of b_1, b_2, and b_3, only one (i.e., b_3 for the ratio of adults in the household roster) was statistically significant at the 5 % level. At most, the balance check only marginally failed for the following four variables: household size, average age, adult ratio, and adult female literacy rate. We can therefore safely conclude that these rejections occurred by chance and that randomization was properly implemented. As shown in Chap. 7, the non-random components at household level do not affect our impact analysis (see the robustness check undertaken by controlling for these four household-level variables that were associated with a marginal failure of the balance check).

5.5 Conclusion

This chapter explained the experimental design of our RCT in northern Bangladesh, which examined the impact of flexible microcredit targeting the ultra-poor. In partnership with GUK, a local NGO with extensive experience in poverty-reduction initiatives in northern Bangladesh, we initiated RCT interventions in 2011 to test the effectiveness of introducing moratoria on monthly repayments during the lean season called *monga*, compared with insistence upon regular and inflexible weekly repayments throughout the year.

In addition to describing our experimental design, this chapter compared the means of the characteristics of sample villages and households across various treatment arms. It revealed that most observable characteristics prior to our intervention were very similar across treatment arms, indicating that randomization was properly implemented. Descriptive analysis of the baseline survey data also showed that our sample households owned very few liquid assets (such as household appliances or livestock) and managed very small land holdings. These findings indicate that our sample households belong to the poorest section of rural Bangladesh.

References

Armendariz B, Morduch J (2010) The economics of microfinance, 2nd edn. MIT Press, Cambridge

Czura K, Karlan D, Mullainathan S (2011) Does flexibility in microfinance pay off? Evidence from a randomized evaluation in rural India. Working paper, October 2011. Goethe University Frankfurt

Feigenberg B, Field E, Pande R (2011) The economic returns to social interaction: experimental evidence from microfinance. Harvard University mimeo

Field E, Pande R (2008) Repayment frequency and default in micro-finance: evidence from India. J Eur Econ Assoc 6(2–3):501–509

Field E, Pande R, Papp J, Jeanette Park Y (2012) Repayment flexibility can reduce financial stress: a randomized control trial with microfinance clients in India. PLoS One 7(9):1–7, e45679

Giné X, Karlan DS (2011) Group versus individual liability: short and long term evidence from Philippine microcredit lending groups. Yale University mimeo

Karlan D, Zinman J (2009) Observing unobservables: identifying information asymmetries with a consumer credit field experiment. Econometrica 77(6):1993–2008

Khandker SR, Mahmud W (2012) Seasonal hunger and public policies: evidence from Northwest Bangladesh. World Bank Publications

Khandker SR (2012) Seasonality of income and poverty in Bangladesh. J Dev Econ 97:244–256

Kurosaki T, Khan HU (2012) Vulnerability of microfinance to strategic default and covariate shocks: evidence from Pakistan. Dev Econ 50(2):81–115

Shoji M (2010) Does contingent repayment in microfinance help the poor during natural disasters? J Dev Stud 46(2):191–210

Shonchoy A (2011) Seasonal migration and micro-credit in the lean period: evidence from Northwest Bangladesh. Institute of Developing Economies mimeo

Chapter 6
Repayment Analysis

Abu S. Shonchoy

Abstract The aim of this chapter is to examine repayment behavior in the context of geographical classification and loan design; we also empirically evaluate the impact of seasonally adjusted microcredit, implemented as per the RCT, to assess the general claims by NGOs vis-à-vis a suspension of loan payments during *monga*. Using both survey and experimental methods, this chapter allows us to see the consequences for both MFIs and the participating borrowers of implementing flexible loan repayment rules during lean periods.

Keywords Microcredit · Default · Seasonality · Consumption smoothing · Bangladesh

6.1 Introduction

A key feature of typical microcredit contracts is an arrangement whereby clients make frequent payments (as often as weekly) within a group setting (Armendariz and Morduch 2005). In an agrarian economy such as that of Bangladesh, the infrequent and seasonally limited opportunities for income within the agricultural sector can make such an arrangement difficult. During lean periods when there are very few jobs available in the rural agricultural sector, it can be especially difficult for the poor to generate income, let alone comply with loan repayment schemes. A rigid weekly repayment schedule during times of seasonal hardship can therefore exacerbate their poverty and suffering.

The lean season, known locally as *monga*, is a distinctive and well-documented feature of life in northern Bangladesh (e.g., Khandker 2012). However,

A. S. Shonchoy (✉)
Institute of Developing Economies, Japan External Trade Organization, 3-2-2 Wakaba Mihama-ku Chiba-shi 261-8545, Japan
e-mail: parves.shonchoy@gmail.com

A. S. Shonchoy (ed.), *Seasonality and Microcredit*, SpringerBriefs in Economics,
DOI: 10.1007/978-4-431-55010-5_6,

microfinance institutions (MFIs) do not offer any sort of seasonally adjusted microcredit product in northern Bangladesh. One could reasonably argue that permitting suspension of weekly repayments of microcredit during *monga* could help poor borrowers to better cope with adverse conditions. However, MFIs believe that weekly collection by loan officers is a key element in the mitigation of loan default risk and that this ultimately makes the poor more viable as borrowers (Field and Pande 2008). In our discussions with various MFIs operating in our project areas, there was universal agreement that seasonal suspension of payments would increase the risk of default and delinquency. Given this trade-off, we implemented a randomized controlled trial (RCT) to evaluate the general claim by NGOs that permitting repayment suspension during *monga* was not viable.

In our experimental design, we first formed 72 groups within two districts in Bangladesh, Gaibandha and Kurigram, chosen because these districts have a long history of *monga*. These 72 groups were randomly allocated to four different intervention treatments.

1. *Flexible 1* (24 villages, 360 households): No payments required during *monga*; after *monga*, regular weekly repayment schedule continues (with slightly higher weekly payments)
2. *Flexible 2* (24 villages, 360 households): Monthly loan repayment during *monga*; after *monga*, return to regular weekly repayments
3. *Flexible 1 + IGA* (12 villages, 180 households): Same as "Flexible 1" above, but in place of a loan, the borrower is given an asset that would otherwise have been purchased with the loan
4. *Control* (24 villages, 360 households): Regular Grameen-type microfinance, with no adjustment for *monga*

In this experiment, our counterpart NGO, Gana Unnayan Kendra (GUK), distributed a BDT 3,000 loan to each household, for a total distribution of BDT 3,240,000 (i.e., BDT 3,000 to each of 1,080 households), with an interest rate of about 17 %. The amount due for each household after a one-year loan cycle (45 installments) was BDT 3,360, for a total loan repayment of BDT 3,628,800. At the time of the survey, the total amount of loan repayments collected was BDT 3,456,388 with BDT 172,412 still outstanding, which is a 95.25 % recovery. Figure 6.1 shows the outstanding loan amount as a percentage of total credit given to each of the treatment groups. We can see that there are no systematic differences among the treatment groups in terms of overdue amounts, even 6 months after the end of the scheduled loan cycle.

The aim of this chapter is to examine repayment behavior in the context of geographical classification and loan design; we also empirically evaluate the impact of seasonally adjusted microcredit, implemented as per the RCT, to assess the general claims by NGOs vis-à-vis a suspension of loan payments during *monga*. Using both survey and experimental methods, this chapter allows us to see the consequences for both MFIs and the participating borrowers of implementing flexible loan repayment rules during lean periods.

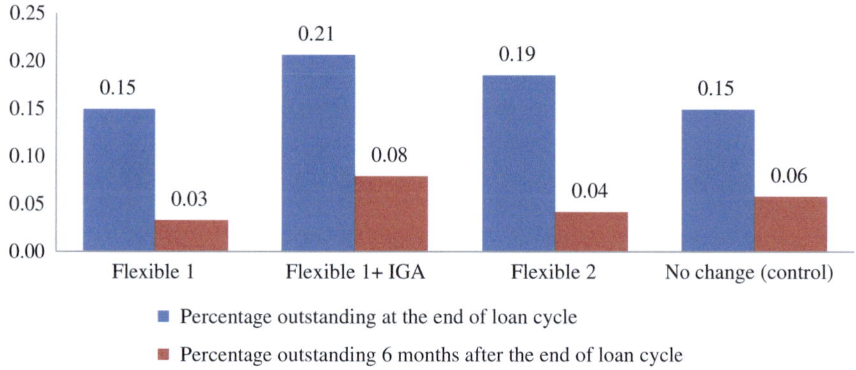

Fig. 6.1 Overdue amount as a percentage of total amount due

6.2 Descriptive Analysis of Default

6.2.1 Geographical Differences

As discussed in Chap. 5, our experimental design allows for the participation of survey villages with three distinct geographical properties. This feature was embedded in the experimental design so that we could better understand how geographical differences influenced things such as people's livelihoods. For instance, in our design, 18 of the 72 sample villages (25.0 % of the sample) are from *char* areas, 42 (58.3 %) are from inland areas, and the remaining 12 (16.7 %) are from river basin areas. In terms of exposure to flooding and erosion, river basins are as vulnerable as *char* areas; however, because of infrastructure for the mitigation of damage from floods and erosion, river basin areas are less vulnerable than *char* areas. In terms of economic opportunities and seasonality, *char* areas are the most vulnerable, as they possess seasonal risks (such as periodic flooding) while income opportunities are limited to only agriculture and small-scale fishing. Hence, *char* households typically face greater difficulty in ensuring a regular flow of income. They also suffer on account of seasonal adversity, as opposed to inland and river basin households, where seasonal adversity is not as severe. This was made apparent during the analysis of repayments by *char* borrowers when compared to those by borrowers in the other two areas. In Fig. 6.2, we plot the mean of default status (*Default* is a dummy variable that is equal to 1 if a borrower's outstanding balance at the end of a loan cycle is positive and 0 otherwise) of sampled households by geographical characteristics. Borrowers who were residents of *char* or river-basin areas were more likely to default or be delinquent when compared with households from inland areas. In terms of the monetary amount of delinquency, mean of overdue amount were almost one-third greater for borrowers from the *char* areas (Fig. 6.3) compared with inland borrowers. Interestingly, 6 months after the end of the scheduled loan cycle, borrowers from

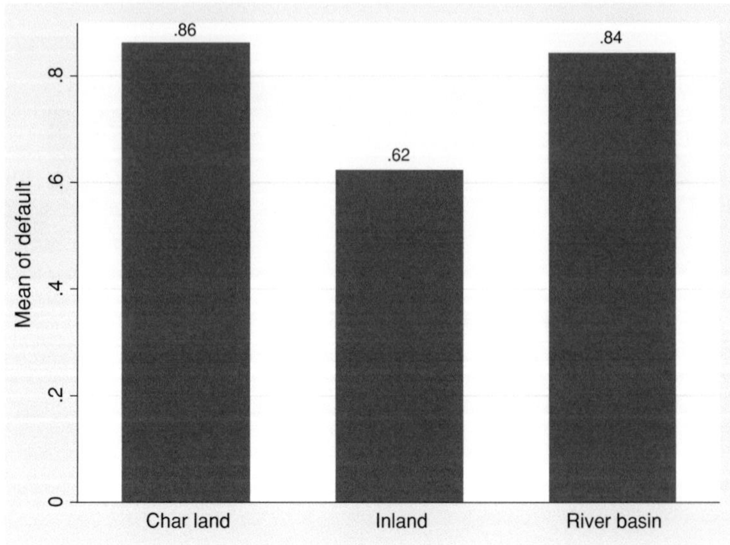

Fig. 6.2 Default analysis by geographical classification

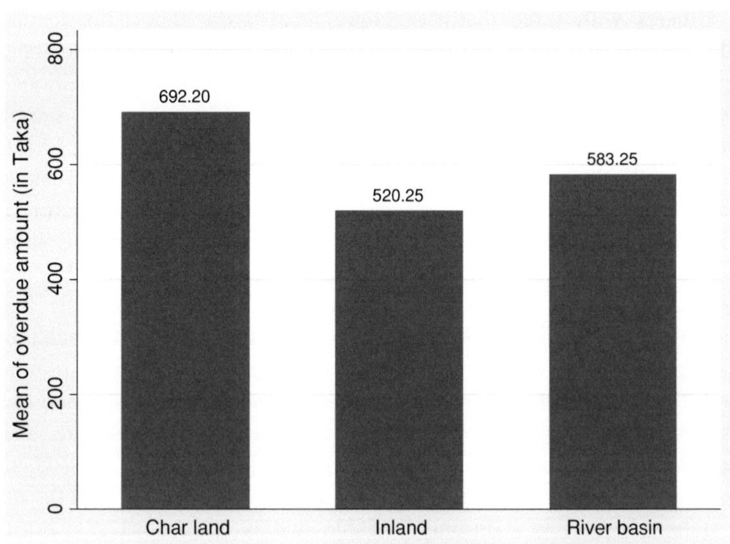

Fig. 6.3 Delinquency analysis by geographical classification

river-basin areas had managed to reduce their delinquent amounts more than borrowers from the other two geographical areas (Fig. 6.4). In Fig. 6.5 we plot the mean of the amount due, as a percentage of the total amount. Here we see that

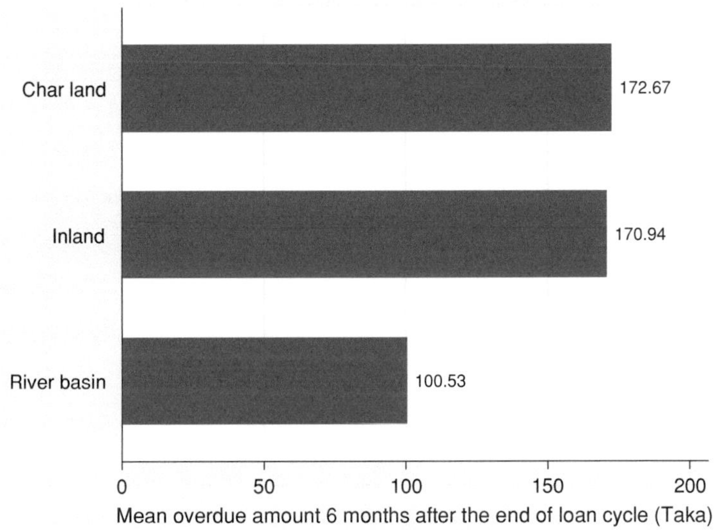

Fig. 6.4 Mean of overdue amount 6 months after end of loan cycle by geographical classification

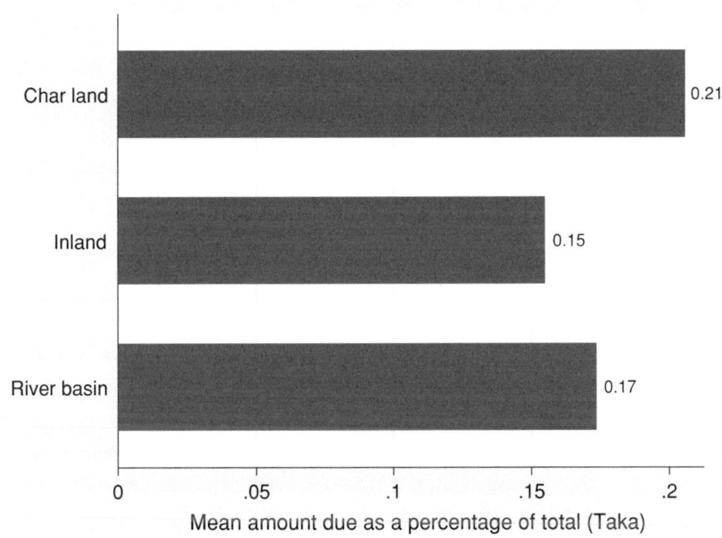

Fig. 6.5 Amount due as a ratio of total amount by geographical classification

delinquent amounts for *char* borrowers were on average about 5 % higher than borrowers of other two geographical regions. This amount, however, fell significantly, 6 months after the end of the scheduled loan cycle, matching the

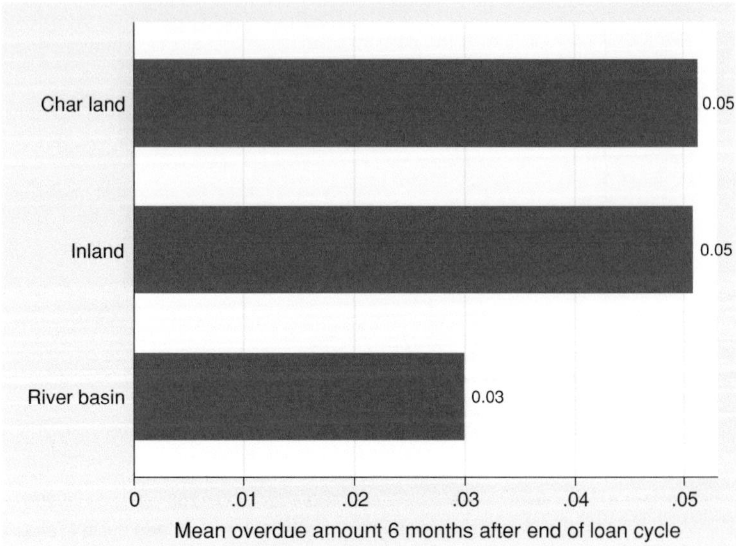

Fig. 6.6 Amount due as a ratio of total amount (6 months after end of loan cycle) by geographical classification

delinquency level of inland borrowers. Inland and *char* borrowers had delinquent amounts of about 5 % while river basin borrowers averaged 3 % of the total amount delinquent (Fig. 6.6). This pattern of higher delinquency by the borrowers from *char* areas are expected as discussed at the beginning of the chapter.

Interestingly, this scenario gets changed when we examine the loan collection record of households from different locations, to check the repayment discipline. As mentioned in previous chapters, MFIs typically impose a strict loan collection discipline where borrowers must make weekly loan payments of equal amounts. However, in our experiment design, we instructed GUK to forgo strict loan repayment discipline. They were instructed to instead conduct weekly household visits and meetings at which borrowers were kept informed of the cumulative due amount. This was done to observe the loan collection pattern and behavior of loan repayment among borrowers. Figure 6.7 depicts the mean of total missed weeks, where a "missed week" is defined as those weeks when a borrower made no payments at all[1] and had not earned any credit toward one or more missed weeks of payments. It is interesting to note that borrowers from river basin areas missed payments the most frequently, missing an average of 7.67 weeks, while inland borrowers performing slightly better at an average of 6.26 weeks missed. *Char* borrowers performed best, with an average of 3.98 weeks of missed payments. The ratio of total missed weeks as a percentage of total loan collection weeks is plotted in Fig. 6.8, which also shows that, on average, river basin borrowers missed 22 %

[1] Any week in which a partial payment was made did not count as a missed week.

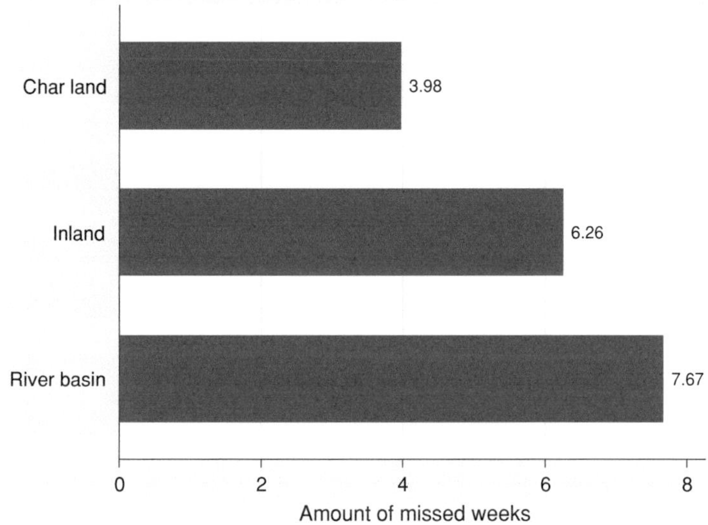

Fig. 6.7 Total missed weeks by geographical classification

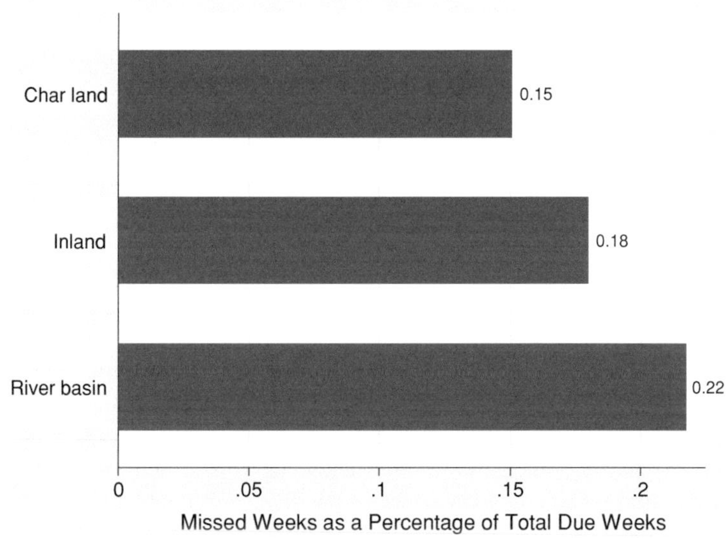

Fig. 6.8 Ratio of missed weeks as a percentage of total weeks by geographical classification

of their scheduled weekly repayments. This figure is about 3 % higher than that for inland borrowers and 6 % higher than that for borrowers from *char* areas. The reason borrowers from *char* areas maintained better discipline than other groups

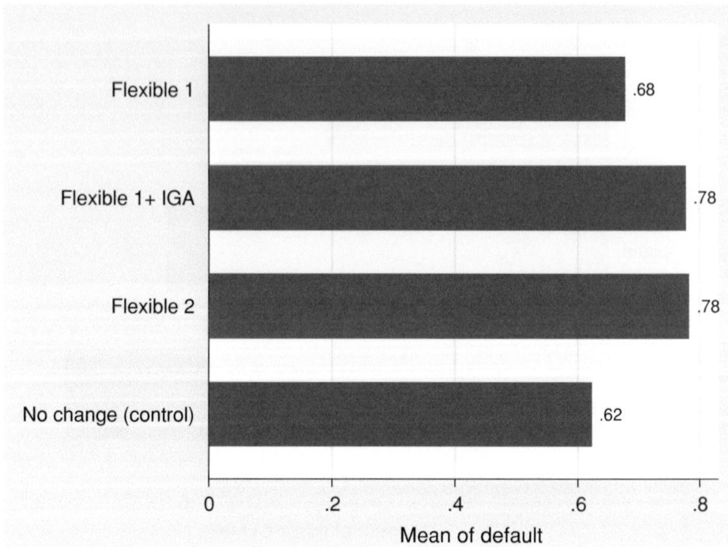

Fig. 6.9 Default rate by treatment classification

perhaps lies in the fact of lacking credit facilities at the *char* areas. MFIs in Bangladesh typically do not extend their credit support to the *char* dwellers, mostly due to the issues like outreach difficulties and vulnerability. As a result, when our counterpart NGO extended their service to the *char* areas due to our designed experiment, borrowers at the *char* showed better discipline behavior, perhaps to assure our NGO that they could also be as disciplined as the borrowers from mainland area.

6.2.2 Treatment Differences

In the treatment-based analysis, we emphasized the seasonally adjusted loan collection pattern of various microcredit contracts that had been implemented randomly among the 72 villages in our sample. In this analysis, the indicator variable *Default* is a dummy variable equal to 1 if a borrower's outstanding balance at the end of the loan cycle is positive, and equal to 0 otherwise. In Fig. 6.9, we see that the control group, which maintained a traditional, rigid weekly repayment scheme, had a relatively lower average rate of default than groups with flexible repayment schemes. However, this indicator variable did not take into account the degree of such loan repayment defaults. To better our understanding of the delinquency amount of various microcredit groups, we need to look at the absolute amount of default, rather than the indicator variables, as the latter provides equal judgment for any positive due amount. Figure 6.10 is such a

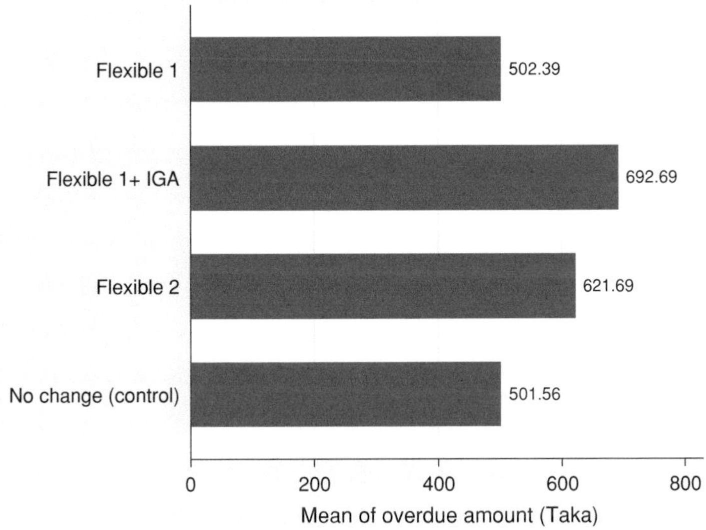

Fig. 6.10 Overdue amounts by treatment classification

diagram detailing various credit treatment groups; it is evident from this diagram that the "Flexible 1 + IGA" treatment arm has a higher absolute amount of delinquency payment than the other groups. As discussed, unlike other groups, the Flexible 1 + IGA group received the income-generating assets (IGA) of their choice within the loan amount, plus IGA-related training, in place of a cash credit. The main reason for such a design is to capture the popular criticism of microcredit—namely, that the credit received by borrowers is largely used in consumption-smoothing, rather than in acquiring assets or undertaking IGAs (e.g., Armendariz and Morduch 2005). However, practitioners of microcredit allow borrowers to smooth consumption, as long as the required weekly due amount are paid on time. In our experimental design, we wanted to test the impact of a restricted consumption-smoothing option with credit, by introducing the "IGA group with loan repayment" pattern, which is similar to that of the "Flexible 1" groups (i.e., complete moratorium during *monga*). Possibly due to the illiquid nature of this treatment arm, we observed a greater rise in delinquency amount in the "Flexible 1 + IGA" group, as the assets they received did not generate enough revenue immediately to allow regular repayments. If we look at the Fig. 6.11, where the ratio of total due amount (as a percentage of total credit amount) has been depicted, we notice that the pattern for "Flexible 1 + IGA" group is the same as noticed before.

To understand the repayment discipline and commitment behavior of various groups, we plotted the mean of the total number of missed weeks in Fig. 6.12. In this figure, the borrowers of the Control group missed, on average, a greater number of weeks than did the other groups. However, these figured do not

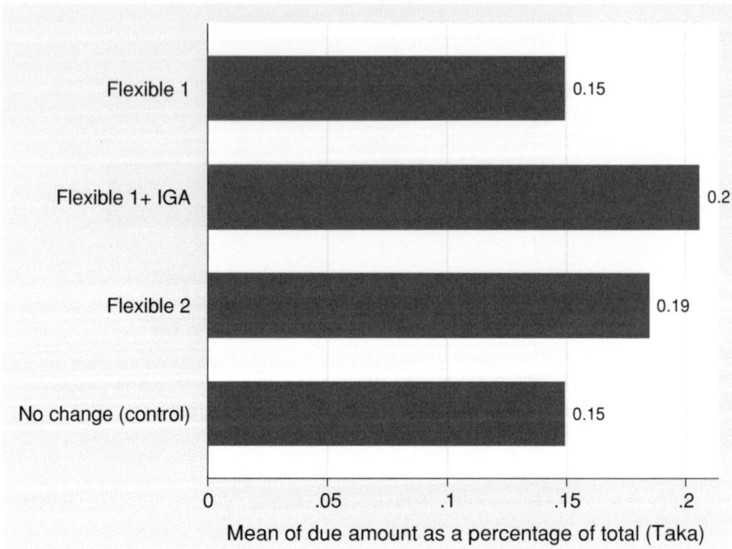

Fig. 6.11 Amount due as a percentage of total amount by treatment classification

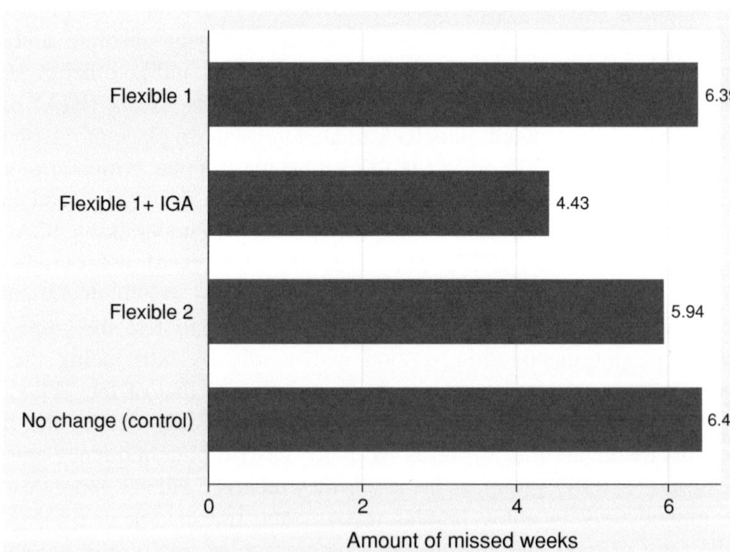

Fig. 6.12 Total missed weeks by treatment classification

represent the true state of the loan discipline pattern, as the Control group had more weekly due (i.e., 45 weeks of repayment obligations) than the other groups (e.g., "Flexible 1" has 36 weeks of repayment obligation). Figure 6.13 depicts the

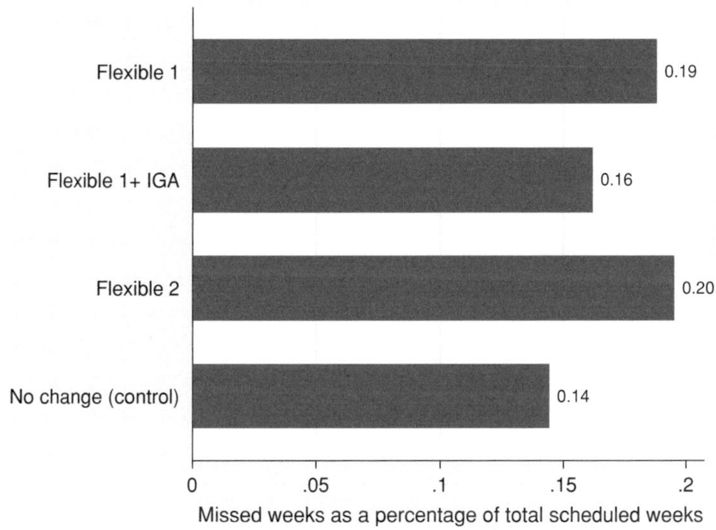

Fig. 6.13 Missed weeks as a percentage of total weeks by treatment classification

mean of the missed weeks as a percentage of total due weeks; it appears that all the flexible groups borrowers had a relatively larger ratio of missed weeks (as a percentage of total weeks), compared to the control group; this is expected and consistent with previous observations.

6.2.3 Seasonality

One important aspect of this analysis is the impact of seasonality on total collection and weekly repayment. To check for seasonal patterns, we plot monthly loan collections and missed weeks as a time series data. In Fig. 6.14, we plot the ratio of monthly collection (as a percentage of total monthly due), based on geographical location. We note that borrowers from various geographical locations possessed almost similar seasonal patterns, albeit with slight variations, in their loan repayment behavior. For example, in terms of better repayment record—which generally reflects a healthy flow of income—both the November–December and May–June periods were favorable months, mostly due to the seasonal earnings that stemmed from paddy harvests. Similarly, most of the underpayments occurred in the off-harvest periods (e.g., October or March–April), thus reflecting the income-smoothing problem faced by the borrowers in these areas, where agriculture is the main source of income. If we were to categorize this analysis based on various credit products (Fig. 6.15), we could see that "Flexible 2" microcredit

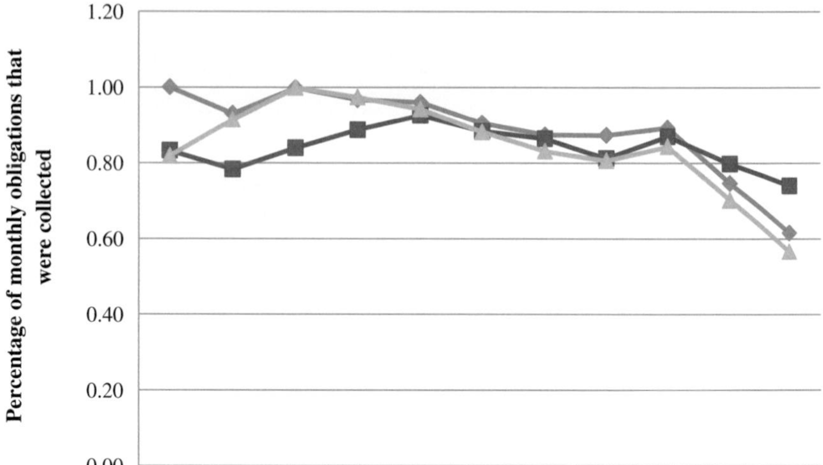

	Sep	Oct	Nov	Dec	Jan	Feb	Mar	Apr	May	Jun	Jul
Char land	1.00	0.93	1.00	0.97	0.96	0.90	0.87	0.87	0.89	0.75	0.62
Inland	0.83	0.78	0.84	0.89	0.93	0.88	0.86	0.81	0.87	0.80	0.74
River basin	0.82	0.91	1.00	0.97	0.94	0.88	0.83	0.81	0.84	0.70	0.57

Fig. 6.14 Monthly collections as a percentage of total monthly amounts due by geographical classification

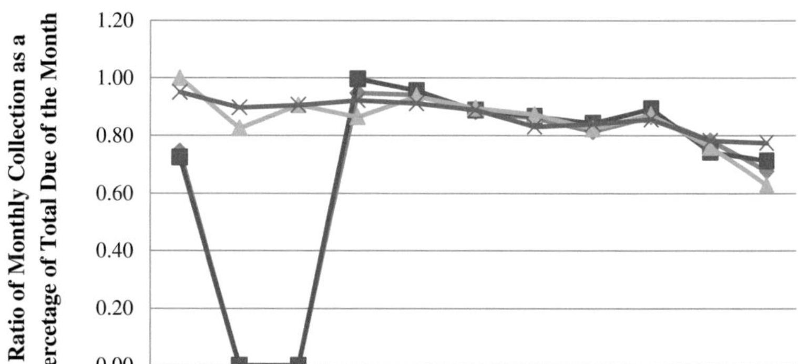

	Sep	Oct	Nov	Dec	Jan	Feb	Mar	Apr	May	Jun	Jul
Flexible 1	0.75	0.00	0.00	0.95	0.94	0.88	0.86	0.81	0.87	0.78	0.68
Flexible 1+ IGA	0.73	0.00	0.00	1.00	0.96	0.89	0.87	0.84	0.89	0.74	0.71
Flexible 2	1.00	0.83	0.91	0.86	0.94	0.90	0.87	0.82	0.87	0.76	0.63
No change (control)	0.95	0.90	0.91	0.92	0.91	0.89	0.83	0.84	0.86	0.78	0.77

Fig. 6.15 Monthly collection as a percentage of total monthly amounts due by treatment classification

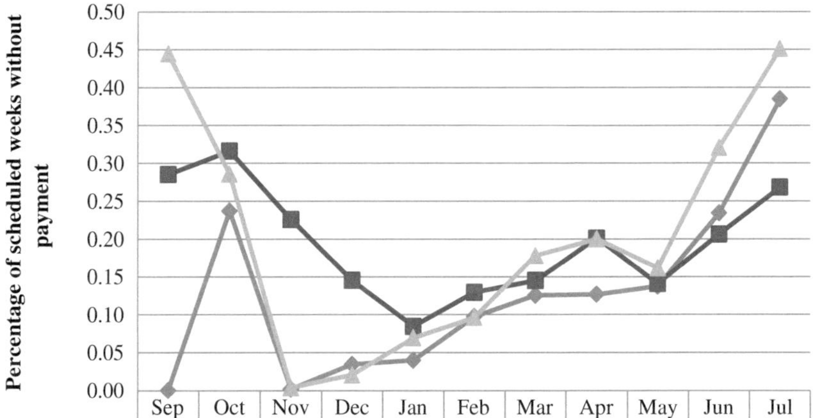

	Sep	Oct	Nov	Dec	Jan	Feb	Mar	Apr	May	Jun	Jul
Char land	0.00	0.24	0.00	0.03	0.04	0.10	0.13	0.13	0.14	0.23	0.38
Inland	0.29	0.32	0.23	0.15	0.08	0.13	0.14	0.20	0.14	0.21	0.27
River basin	0.44	0.29	0.00	0.02	0.07	0.10	0.18	0.20	0.16	0.32	0.45

Fig. 6.16 Missed weeks as a percentage of total scheduled weeks by geographical classification

borrowers in most months underpaid their required loan repayment amounts, compared with other borrowing groups. However, distinct adverse periods like *monga* (late September to late November) affect all groups, irrespective of flexibility. Similar patterns could be observed before and after the harvest of the Boro paddy in the April–May and June–July seasons, respectively.

In terms of weekly collection and understanding the discipline framework imposed by the MFIs, we see almost similar trends among the borrowing groups of various geographical locations (Fig. 6.16). As these groups reached the end of the loan cycle, they tended to miss more weekly payments, compared to the beginning part of the loan collection period. However, one interesting observation to note is that the ratio of missed weeks to the total monthly due weeks was still lower in November–January and in May, which could be attributed to the paddy harvest cycles, as previously observed. In Fig. 6.17 we see a pattern similar to that observed before, where we plot the same ratio of missed weeks (as a percentage of total due weeks) by loan product classification. It appears that the "Flexible 2" had, on average, the highest ratio of missed weeks in most months, and the "Flexible 1 + IGA" group had the lowest.

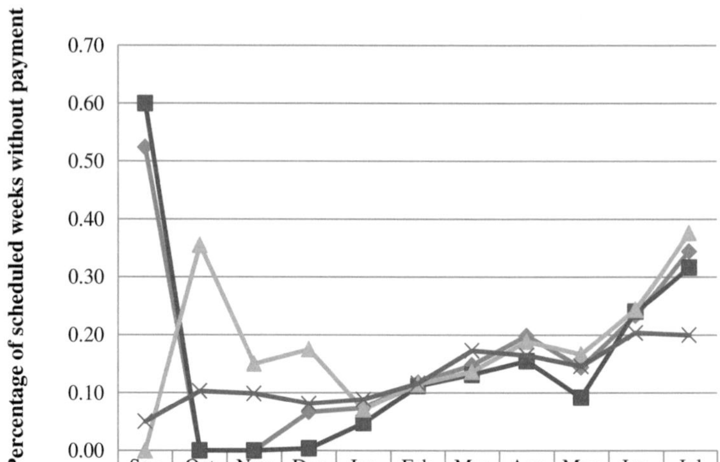

	Sep	Oct	Nov	Dec	Jan	Feb	Mar	Apr	May	Jun	Jul
Flexible 1	0.52	0.00	0.00	0.07	0.07	0.12	0.15	0.20	0.14	0.23	0.34
Flexible 1+ IGA	0.60	0.00	0.00	0.00	0.05	0.11	0.13	0.16	0.09	0.24	0.32
Flexible 2	0.00	0.36	0.15	0.18	0.07	0.12	0.14	0.19	0.17	0.24	0.38
No Change (control)	0.05	0.10	0.10	0.08	0.09	0.12	0.17	0.16	0.15	0.20	0.20

Fig. 6.17 Missed weeks as a percentage of total scheduled weeks by treatment classification

6.3 Econometric Analysis of Defaults

6.3.1 Empirical Strategy

Since loan treatments were randomly assigned (see Chap. 5), to empirically complement our discussion of the repayment analysis, we can use ordinary least squares (OLS) regression to evaluate the impact of various treatments on a number of outcomes. More precisely, we can estimate the same regression as estimated in Chap. 5 for the current analysis. We estimate

$$Y_h = b_0 + b_1 D_{1h} + b_2 D_{2h} + b_3 D_{3h} + u_h, \tag{6.1}$$

where Y_h is the outcome variable for household h, D_{jh} ($j = 1, 2, 3$) is a dummy variable indicating that household h was provided flexible microcredit under treatment condition j ($j = 1, 2, 3$; these correspond to Flexible 1, Flexible 1 + IGA, and Flexible 2, respectively), and u_h is a zero mean error term. Because the randomization was implemented at the village level and sample households were drawn from the village as the primary sampling unit, we used robust standard errors for b's cluster at the village level when testing the null hypothesis.

6.3.2 Impact of Flexibility on Repayment Behavior

As mentioned in the introduction, our main motivation in introducing seasonally adjusted flexible microcredit was to verify the rationale of the MFIs working in northern Bangladesh for not providing flexibility in loan repayment during *monga*. The reluctance of MFIs to provide flexibility or seasonal adjustments during *monga* is attributed to mainly two reasons: (1) it might break the borrowers' loan collection discipline, and (2) it might increase the rate of loan default. When we introduced this experimental design, our NGO counterpart GUK strongly argued that the loan default rate would increase significantly in the most flexible group (Flexible 1): they believed it would hamper loan discipline and also affect borrowers' financial behavior vis-à-vis the making of regular installment payments. Some GUK executives also said that borrowers from the most flexible group might "run away" with the money.

To determine the validity of these claims, we performed regression analysis based on the loan collection data of GUK. The summary statistics of the data is depicted in Table 6.1 whereas the regression results are reported in Table 6.2 where simple OLS regressions results of various outcomes of interests, with village-level clustered standard errors in parentheses. From column (1) to column (5), our results are strongly uniform; we found no systematic differences among the various indicators of loan default, delinquency amount, or missed weeks among the various treatment groups when compared with traditional microcredit borrowers—most of whom are in favor of a flexible microcredit design. The null hypothesis that $b_1 = b_2 = b_3 = 0$ was not rejected, even at the 10 % level, indicating that the flexibility in our RCT had no impact on households' repayment behavior. This finding has important policy implications vis-à-vis the design of microcredit schemes. Contrary to the claims of MFIs in Bangladesh, we saw no statistically significant differences among the treatment conditions. In the treatment condition featuring a complete suspension of weekly repayment during *monga* (high-risk credit) and monthly repayment during *monga* (low-risk credit), we found no statistically significant pattern of delinquency or less frequent repayment, despite the MFI claims of increased problems with discipline and repayment. It appears that even when imposing a high level of credit risk (Flexible 1) on our counterpart MFI, GUK did not face a level of delinquency that was statistically significantly different from the delinquency amount seen among groups offered traditional microcredit product (the delinquency rates were 6 % and 3 % in the cases of traditional and Flexible 1 borrowing, respectively).

6.3.3 Impression of Flexible Microcredit

To understand borrowers' reactions to the current repayment flexibility experiment and their feedback with respect to it, we conducted a satisfaction survey much like that of Devoto et al. (2012), who asked existing clients whether they had any

Table 6.1 Descriptive statistics

Variables	Mean	SD	Min	Max
Dummy for default (1 if due amount is positive)	0.72	0.45	0	1
Total amount of outstanding at the end of loan cycle	573.74	630.89	0	3,285
Ratio of outstanding amount as a percentage of total due amount	0.17	0.19	0	1
Total number of missed weeks	5.92	6.60	0	41
Total amount of outstanding six months after the loan cycle	159.64	501.93	0	3,210
Ratio of missed weeks as a percentage of total due weeks	0.18	0.18	0	1
Ratio of September collection as a percentage of September due	0.85	0.23	0	1
Ratio of October collection as a percentage of October due	0.84	0.27	0	1
Ratio of November collection as a percentage of November due	0.91	0.26	0	1
Ratio of December collection as a percentage of December due	0.92	0.25	0	1
Ratio of January collection as a percentage of January due	0.94	0.17	0	1
Ratio of February collection as a percentage of February due	0.89	0.23	0	1
Ratio of March collection as a percentage of March due	0.86	0.26	0	1
Ratio of April collection as a percentage of April due	0.83	0.28	0	1
Ratio of May collection as a percentage of May due	0.87	0.25	0	1
Ratio of June collection as a percentage of June due	0.77	0.32	0	1
Ratio of July collection as a percentage of July due	0.68	0.38	0	1
Ratio of missed weeks as a percentage of total due weeks in September	0.28	0.35	0	1
Ratio of missed weeks as a percentage of total due weeks in October	0.29	0.44	0	1
Ratio of missed weeks as a percentage of total due weeks in November	0.13	0.33	0	1
Ratio of missed weeks as a percentage of total due weeks in December	0.10	0.29	0	1
Ratio of missed weeks as a percentage of total due weeks in January	0.07	0.18	0	1
Ratio of missed weeks as a percentage of total due weeks in February	0.12	0.24	0	1
Ratio of missed weeks as a percentage of total due weeks in March	0.15	0.27	0	1
Ratio of missed weeks as a percentage of total due weeks in April	0.18	0.29	0	1
Ratio of missed weeks as a percentage of total due weeks in May	0.15	0.27	0	1
Ratio of missed weeks as a percentage of total due weeks in June	0.23	0.33	0	1
Ratio of missed weeks as a percentage of total due weeks in July	0.33	0.39	0	1

SD stands for Standard Deviation

complaints, problems, or difficulties with the assigned treatment schedule of repayment. In the current study, if the borrower responded affirmatively, then we categorized such an answer as "not satisfied" in the satisfaction index and as 0 otherwise.

Basic regression estimates are presented in columns (1)–(4) of Table 6.3. Columns (1) and (2) use the entire sample; columns (3) and (4) use the sample of direct beneficiaries (1,080 households in total). Our preferred estimation is that in column (4), where one can clearly observe that borrowers under the Flexible 1 repayment scheme (complete suspension of repayment requirements during *monga*) were more likely to report positively than those who borrowed under the typical microcredit repayment scheme (regular weekly repayment). Among the treatments, Flexible 1 had a higher level of satisfaction than the other similar groups; this finding is consistent with our hypothesis.

Table 6.2 Regression analysis

	(1) Total outstanding amount	(2) Default	(3) Total number of missed weeks	(4) Ratio of missed weeks (percentage of total weeks)	(5) Ratio of due as a percentage of total due
Flexible 1	0.836	0.056	−0.050	0.044	0.000
	(185.233)	(0.130)	(2.420)	(0.055)	(0.055)
Flexible 1 + IGA	191.139	0.156	−2.006	0.018	0.057
	(258.780)	(0.151)	(2.350)	(0.063)	(0.077)
Flexible 2	120.139	0.161	−0.494	0.051	0.036
	(192.997)	(0.126)	(2.341)	(0.053)	(0.057)
Constant	501.556***	0.622***	6.439***	0.144***	0.149***
	(169.025)	(0.105)	(2.137)	(0.045)	(0.050)
N	1,080	1,080	1,080	1,080	1,080
R-squared	0.0143	0.0203	0.0112	0.0107	0.0143
F-stat. for zero slopes of all dummies	0.53	0.75	0.73	0.39	0.53

Note Robust standard errors, clustered at the village level, are shown in brackets
Significance at the 10 % (*), 5 % (**), and 1 % (***) levels
Source Estimated by the author, using the microdata described in the text

Table 6.3 Regression estimation for satisfaction survey

	(1)	(2)	(3)	(4)
Flexible 1	0.287***	0.287**	0.303***	0.303**
	(0.043)	(0.125)	(0.044)	(0.124)
Flexible 2	0.211***	0.211*	0.206***	0.206
	(0.044)	(0.126)	(0.045)	(0.128)
Flexible 1 + IGA	0.116**	0.116	0.106**	0.106
	(0.051)	(0.163)	(0.053)	(0.163)
Constant	0.467***	0.467***	0.456***	0.456***
	(0.037)	(0.103)	(0.037)	(0.104)
N	1,146	1,146	1,080	1,080
Village clustered S.E.	No	Yes	No	Yes
Sample	All	All	Only borrower	Only borrower
R	0.044	0.044	0.05	0.05
Adjusted R	0.041	0.041	0.047	0.047

Note Robust standard errors clustered at the village level are shown in brackets
Significant at the 10 % (*), 5 % (**), and 1 % (***) levels
Source Estimated by the author, using the microdata described in the text

6.4 Conclusion

In this chapter, we used both descriptive and empirical analyses to examine repayment behavior among borrowers from various geographical locations with different levels of exposure to seasonal vulnerability and among borrowers with access to various microcredit products, which were assigned to them under the RCT-based field experimental framework. Our aim in this chapter was to rigorously delimit the relative frequency of repayment and relative delinquency of borrowers of various classifications. Our descriptive analyses suggest that borrowers facing seasonality in various locations show similar patterns of repayment behavior; however, the vulnerability, seasonality, and adversity faced by *char* dwellers are of an extreme nature, and this is reflected in the repayment patterns of borrowers from *char* areas. We noticed that *char* dwellers were on average better disciplined in following the loan repayment framework, but still underperformed in terms of paying their regular weekly dues. In contrast, borrowers from river basin areas had difficulty following the weekly repayment discipline, but this group did comparatively well in terms of repaying the total due amount. Moreover, our descriptive analyses of various microcredit products suggest that the provision of illiquid microcredit (where an asset is provided in place of liquid credit) may not be able to immediately promote income generating activities. In fact, we found patterns of slightly increased default risk and marginally greater monetary delinquency within the "Flexible 1 + IGA" treatment than in groups receiving the other loan products. It appears that the "Flexible 1 + IGA" group performed well in following the loan discipline; however, this group, on average, may had difficulty in making the full weekly repayment on each week.

In the empirical analysis contained within this chapter, we tested the general opinions of microfinance practitioners in Bangladesh, who do not offer seasonality-adjusted microcredit products. These MFIs' rationale in not providing any flexibility or seasonal adjustments during *monga* is twofold: (1) it might break borrowers' loan repayment discipline and (2) it might increase loan defaults. As part of an RCT-based field experiment in northern Bangladesh, we randomly assigned seasonally adjusted flexible microcredit and traditional rigid microcredit to various borrowing groups. Our observation suggest that there are no systematic differences among the treatment groups in terms of default or overdue amount, and these findings thus support the provision of a flexible microcredit design. Even after allowing a more flexible payment schedule and seasonal suspension of payments, we found that our counterpart NGO managed to obtain more than 95 % of its maximal payment of principal and interest, and so this can be considered a successful business microfinance model.

References

Armendariz B, Morduch J (2005) The economics of microfinance. MIT Press, Cambridge

Devoto F, Duflo E, Dupas P, Parienté W, Pons V (2012) Happiness on tap: piped water adoption in urban Morocco. Am Econ J Econ Policy 4(4):68–99

Field E, Pande R (2008) Repayment frequency and default in microfinance: evidence from India. J Eur Econ Assoc 6(2–3):501–509

Khandker SR (2012) Seasonality of income and poverty in Bangladesh. J Dev Econ 97(2):244–256

Chapter 7
Impact of Flexible Microcredit on Food Consumption

Takashi Kurosaki

Abstract This chapter empirically assesses whether a flexible repayment design for microcredit can enhance food consumption among the ultra-poor. Using a cross-section dataset collected in northern Bangladesh in 2011–2012, we find that repayment flexibility does not have a positive impact on food consumption during or immediately after the period under the randomized controlled trial intervention. However, all microcredit borrowers tended to have more secure food consumption than non-borrowers. We provide several interpretations for the insignificant impact of the repayment flexibility, such as the difficulty for households to smooth consumption across seasons, a long period required for the income gain to realize, or the treated households' perception of the transient nature of the intervention.

Keywords Microcredit · Randomized controlled trial · Seasonality · Food security · Bangladesh

7.1 Introduction

This chapter empirically investigates whether the ultra-poor can fully utilize the opportunities arising from a relaxed microcredit repayment scheme. As shown in the preceding chapters, Chaps. 3 and 4 in particular, seasonal deprivation associated with *monga* (the agriculturally lean season between transplanting and harvest of *Aman* paddy, the main rice variety) is a serious threat to the poor of Bangladesh. In northern Bangladesh, where poverty is deeper than in other regions of the country, the poor usually go to extremes in order to cope with such seasonality. However, microcredit providers in northern Bangladesh do not offer any

T. Kurosaki (✉)
Hitotsubashi University, 2-1 Naka, Kunitachi, Tokyo 186-8603, Japan
e-mail: kurosaki@ier.hit-u.ac.jp

A. S. Shonchoy (ed.), *Seasonality and Microcredit*, SpringerBriefs in Economics,
DOI: 10.1007/978-4-431-55010-5_7, © IDE-JETRO 2014

special loan products designed to cope with the difficulties of *monga*. The typical loan products offered in northern Bangladesh are rigid Grameen-style microcredit schemes with strictly enforced and equally sized weekly installment payments. Given the scarcity of informal jobs in the agricultural sector during *monga* and a very limited nonagricultural sector, it is very difficult for the poor to generate income; therefore, a rigid weekly repayment schedule during the time of seasonal hardship exacerbates their suffering. It was found that during *monga*, households used extreme coping measures such as skipping regular meals. One hypothesis we will test in this chapter, therefore, is that the relaxation of loan repayment terms during *monga* increases meal regularity and helps to abate seasonal starvation.

To test this hypothesis, in early 2011 we initiated a randomized experiment in northern Bangladesh (see Chap. 5). In this chapter, we empirically investigate whether flexible microcredit is more effective than traditional, inflexible microcredit in allowing borrower households to increase their consumption levels. For this purpose, we employ a cross-section dataset collected in northern Bangladesh in 2012, after our randomized controlled trial (RCT) was implemented in 2011–2012 (Fig. 5.1).

In Sect. 7.2, we briefly review our RCT design and data. Section 7.3 explains the empirical strategy for the impact assessment. Section 7.4 details the impact of the RCT on food consumption. As a preview of the results, we find that repayment flexibility does not have a positive impact on food consumption during or immediately after the period under the RCT intervention. We interpret these findings in the concluding section of this chapter.

7.2 The Experiment and Data Used

7.2.1 RCT of Flexible Microcredit

We implemented the RCT in collaboration with a nongovernment organization (NGO) known as Gana Unnayan Kendra (GUK). GUK is a local NGO based in Gaibandha district in northern Bangladesh, where the population of the ultra-poor is high because of severe *monga* and frequent flooding from the Jamuna River (Chap. 4).

Out of 90 villages under potential treatment by the counterpart NGO, we randomly selected 12 villages to act as a control group, to which traditional, inflexible microcredit was given, and 60 other villages were offered various types of flexible microcredit schemes. In each of these 72 villages, a borrower group known as a *samity* was formed, comprising 20 members who satisfied the NGO's microcredit criteria and had been identified as being interested in receiving microcredit. Of these members, 15 were given microcredit loans of

BDT 3,000[1] in September 2011, while the remaining members did not receive microcredit in 2011–2012.

In the control villages, borrowers began repayment after a 2-week grace period. Repayments were made in 45 installments, each of which was BDT75 (except for final payment, which was BDT 60), implying a gross interest payment of BDT 360 spread across the borrowing period of approximately 1 year. Each of the weekly installments was to be repaid at a weekly meeting by the borrower: the borrower was obliged to attend the weekly meeting, even during *monga*.

Of the 60 villages that were offered flexible microcredit schemes, 24 were offered the first treatment, "Flexible 1," in which the repayment was temporarily suspended during the designated *monga* period (September 20 to December 20). During the *monga* period, the Flexible 1 group members made no installment payments. After the *monga* period, the borrowers began paying BDT 100 per week, so that their total repayment amount and repayment period were identical to those of the control group.

As a variant of the first treatment, 12 villages were offered Flexible 1 payment terms supplemented with income-generation activities (IGA) support. We refer to this treatment as "Flexible 1 + IGA." In this group, instead of being given cash, microcredit borrowers were provided with their choice of a productive asset, within the credit amount, and advice on how best to utilize that asset. However, no further subsidy was provided.

The second flexibility treatment was offered to 24 villages. Under this treatment arm, the repayment scheme was changed to three monthly installments of BDT 300 during the designated *monga* period, replacing the 12 weekly repayments of BDT 75 each. After the *monga* period was over, borrowers resumed paying BDT 75 per week, so that their total repayment amount and repayment period were identical to those of the control group. We refer to this treatment as "Flexible 2."

The first row of Table 7.1 shows the distribution of sample villages by treatment arms. We randomly assigned one of the four arms to villages, stratified by distance from the closest bus station and by village location type (*char*,[2] river basin, or inland). As shown in Chap. 5, the randomization was properly implemented.

The second panel of Table 7.1 shows the distribution of sample households across various treatment arms. Because one-fourth of our sample households did not receive microcredit, the full 1,440-household sample is partitioned into Flexible 1, Flexible 1 + IGA, Flexible 2, Control, or non-borrower households. As shown in Chap. 5, there were few systematic differences among these five categories of households.

---

[1] As mentioned in an earlier chapter, BDT 100 is equivalent to approximately JPY 99 or USD 1.22. Therefore, BDT 3,000 equaled approximately USD 37.

[2] *Char*, which literally means "river island," is an area of land regularly formed from river bed sediment that has been eroded by the major rivers of Bangladesh. People living on *char* islands tend to be poorer and more vulnerable to various types of natural disasters (see Chap. 4).

Table 7.1 Distribution of sample villages and households by treatment type, northern Bangladesh, 2011

	Treatment allocation at the village level				Total
	Flexible 1	Flexible 1 + IGA	Flexible 2	Control	
Number of villages	24	12	24	12	72
Number of households in the baseline survey, 2011 (Panel 1)					
Borrower	360	180	360	180	1,080
Non-borrower	120	60	120	60	360
Total	480	240	480	240	1,440
Number of households in the resurvey, 2012 (Panel 3)					
Borrower	356	176	356	180	1,068
Non-borrower	117	59	118	60	344
Total	473	235	474	240	1,422

Source Compiled by the author

7.2.2 Microdata Used in the Impact Evaluation

In July–August 2012, we implemented a resurvey of the 1,440 households that were covered in the baseline survey conducted in July–August 2011. This survey, referred to as Panel 3, details information on the household roster; education; health, including the weights of children; occupation; assets; income; migration experiences; agricultural production; nonagricultural enterprises; saving; credit; debt; *monga* coping strategies; changes within the last 12 months; and similar characteristics.

We were able to resurvey 1,422 households, implying an attrition rate of 1.25 %. Although this rate is low, we must consider the possibility of attrition bias (i.e., if attrition occurred nonrandomly). In the third panel of Table 7.1, we show the distribution of resurveyed households across different treatment arms. As shown in the table, attrition occurred among households in villages under Flexible 1, Flexible 1 + IGA, and Flexible 2 treatment arms, but there was no attrition among households in the control villages. According to chi-squared tests, the dropout dummy and the treatment status were independent.[3] Furthermore, the village and household characteristics that were found to be marginally correlated with the treatment in Chap. 5 held no explanatory power when we regressed the dropout dummy on these variables (see Appendix, Table 7.7). We therefore conclude that the resurvey data can be used in the impact evaluation without fear of attrition bias.

---

[3] We first tested the independence between the attrition dummy and five household statuses (Flexible 1, Flexible 1 + IGA, Flexible 2, Control, and Non-borrower). The chi-squared statistics with the degree of freedom (d.o.f.) 4 was 4.257, whose p-value was 0.370. We then tested the same null hypothesis, excluding control households because there was no attrition among this group. The chi-squared statistics with d.o.f. 3 was 1.4654, whose p-value was 0.690.

Table 7.2 Definitions and summary statistics of household-level variables used in the impact analysis, northern Bangladesh, 2011–2012

Variable	Definition	N	Mean	SD	Min	Max
Food Consumption during *monga* 2011						
num_mong1	Number of stomach-full meals per day during *monga* 2011	1,414	2.114	0.411	1	3
num_mong2	Number of minimum stomach-full meals per day during *monga* 2011	1,412	1.693	0.498	1	3
safe_mong	Dummy for food safety during *monga* 2011 (defined as *num_mong2* = 2 or 3)	1,412	0.676	0.468	0	1
meat_mong	Dummy for having meat within a month during *monga* 2011	1,414	0.756	0.430	0	1
Food Consumption during non-*monga* times in 2012						
num_norm1	Number of stomach-full meals per day during non-*monga* times in 2012	1,416	2.859	0.362	1	3
num_norm2	Number of minimum stomach-full meals per day during non-*monga* times in 2012	1,415	2.127	0.586	1	3
safe_norm	Dummy for food safety during non-*monga* times in 2012 (defined as *num_norm2* = 2 or 3)	1,415	0.885	0.319	0	1

Note Mean and standard deviations are unweighted. The question "Number of (minimum) stomach-full meals in a day" was asked of respondents, who reported a typical number, so the answer took an integer value of either 1, 2, or 3
Source Compiled by the author from 2012 resurvey data (Panel 3)

Table 7.2 describes seven qualitative measures of food consumption that we will analyze in this chapter.[4] During *monga* in 2011,[5] many households were unable to have three stomach-full meals each day. The average number of meals (*num_mong1*) was 2.1 meals per day; this fell as low as 1.7 meals a day during the worst days of *monga* (*num_mong2*). A dummy variable (*safe_mong*) was given the value of 1 if the household could always afford 2 or 3 meals per day, even during the worst period; this is used as a measure of food security. Using this measure, 68 % of the households were food-secure during *monga* 2011. As another measure of food security, we use a dummy variable for meat consumption within any month during the *monga* of 2011. 66 % of sample households were able to eat some meat.[6]

---

[4] Quantitative information on household consumption—such as total expenditure, including the imputed value of self-produced foods—is not available in our dataset.

[5] Information on food consumption during *monga* 2011 was collected in the Panel 3 survey, which covered the entire *monga* period; this information, therefore, is not the same as that on food consumption, which was collected during *monga* 2011 (i.e., in the Panel 2 survey in November 2011) and analyzed in Chap. 4. The results reported in this chapter remain qualitatively the same if we use Panel 2 survey data instead.

[6] In the questionnaire, we also asked about fish consumption. The absolute majority of sample households were able to eat fish each month, even during *monga*. Given this lack of variation, we use meat as a measure of protein security.

As shown in the last panel of Table 7.2, food consumption situations improved substantially after *monga*. The average number of stomach-full meals per day during the normal, non-*monga* time in 2012 (*num_norm1*) was 2.9; during the worst days of that period, this number fell slightly to 2.1 meals a day (*num_norm2*). Using *safe_norm*, a dummy variable that takes the value of 1 if the household could afford 2 or 3 meals per day, we find that even during the worst period, 89 % of households were food-secure during normal non-*monga* times in 2012. Although not shown in the table, almost all sample households were able to consume some meat during a given month; therefore, for the impact analysis of food consumption during this period, we will use only *num_norm2* and *safe_norm* as dependent variables.

7.3 Empirical Strategy

Because the intervention was randomly assigned (see Chap. 5), we simply regressed the Panel 3 outcomes on the dummy variables for various treatments. More precisely, we estimated

$$Y_h = b_0 + b_1 D_{1h} + b_2 D_{2h} + b_3 D_{3h} + b_4 D_{4h} + u_h, \qquad (7.1)$$

where Y_h is a post-intervention outcome variable for household h, D_{jh} ($j = 1, 2, 3$) is a dummy variable indicating that household h was provided with flexible microcredit under treatment arm j($j = 1, 2, 3$; these correspond to Flexible 1, Flexible 1 + IGA, and Flexible 2, respectively), D_{4h} is a dummy for non-borrower households, and u_h is a zero mean error term. If the null hypothesis that $b_1 = b_2 = b_3 = 0$ is not rejected, it indicates that the flexibility had no impact. If this null hypothesis is not rejected while another null hypothesis $b_4 = 0$ is rejected, it indicates that microcredit provision had an impact, regardless of flexibility. If the null hypothesis that $b_1 = b_2 = b_3 = 0$ is rejected, we will attempt to determine which flexibility scheme was most effective by comparing the three parameters b_1, b_2, and b_3. Because the randomization was implemented at the village level and sample households were selected from the village as a primary sampling unit, we use robust standard errors for b's, clustered at the village level, to test the null hypotheses.

Although randomization is expected to result in the treatment and control households being similar across all variables, within any particular sample there can be small baseline differences (see Chap. 5). To address this, we added a control for baseline variables that were associated with significant differences across treatments to Eq. (7.1). We will use this as a robustness check. Other specifications including the use of changes in outcomes between Panels 3 and 1 as dependent variables are left for future research.

We estimated two further models to use as additional robustness checks. In the first model, the last term in Eq. (7.1), $b_4 D_{4h}$, was allowed to have various slopes depending on the village-level treatment type. If there were spillover effects from borrowers to non-borrower households within a *samity*, and these effects were systematically different, depending on the treatment arm assigned to the 180 *samity*, then non-borrower households could be heterogeneous across the village-level treatment arms. The extended model can accommodate this possibility. In the second model, we dropped the last term in Eq. (7.1), b_4D_{4h}, and estimated the contracted model using data on borrower households only.

7.4 Impact on Food Consumption

7.4.1 Expected Signs of Parameter Estimates

To examine the impact of repayment flexibility on food consumption, we estimated Eq. (7.1) by using each of the six variables listed in Table 7.2 (*num_mong1*, *num_mong2*, *safe_mong*, *meat_mong*, *num_norm2*, *safe_norm*) as dependent variables. As stated previously, due to a lack of variation, the variable *num_norm1* in Table 7.2 was not analyzed.

Theoretically speaking, the impact of repayment flexibility on food consumption is indirect. The flexibility does not directly affect the ways in which households choose consumption. However, it does indirectly affect consumption through income, price, and credit constraint effects.

We begin with the discussion of the likely sign of b_4. We expect it to be negative, indicating that the provision of microcredit increases food consumption. The first channel is the income effect. If microcredit enhances permanent household income by allowing households to allocate resources more efficiently, the resulting increase in income should be reflected in higher levels of food consumption. This should apply to each of the six dependent variables. The second channel is the price effect. If microcredit enhances the productivity of self-employment and there is imperfection in labor markets, the shadow price of family labor should increase, which is, in turn, likely to lead to the allocation of more household resources to food (as the major input to human capital). However, it is also possible that an increase in the shadow wage could move the demand for food consumption in the *opposite* direction. Theoretically, the net impact can be either positive or negative, but in either case, the absolute value of the net impact is not likely to be large. The third channel is the credit constraint effect. By definition, the provision of microcredit to a household enhances its ability to smooth resource allocation across time. Since *monga* suffering is anticipated by households, it is possible that reducing food consumption during *monga* is a symptom of a binding liquidity constraint. If this is the case, we expect b_4 to be more negative when the dependent variables are those for food consumption during *monga* than those for the normal time following *monga*.

If the flexible arrangements examined in our experiments have similar magnitudes of income, price, and credit effects, we expect each of b_1, b_2, and b_3 to be zero. Alternatively, if Flexible 1 + IGA makes it more likely for borrower households to engage in self-employment businesses that yield immediate gains, the income and price effects are likely to be larger for this treatment than for others. If this is the case, we expect b_2 to be positive and larger than each of b_1 and b_3. With regard to the liquidity effect, we expect Flexible 1 and Flexible 1 + IGA to show additional gains over Flexible 2 and for Flexible 2 to have additional gains over the control group. This is because the suspension of repayment gives households greater freedom in allocating money across the 60 days of *monga* than the inflexible, traditional microcredit scheme; similarly, monthly repayments give households more freedom to allocate money across the 28 days within a month of *monga* than traditional microcredit. If this is the case, we expect $b_1 = b_2 > b_3 > 0$.

7.4.2 Estimation Results

The results regarding the impact of our RCT on food consumption during *monga* 2011 are reported in Table 7.3. For all four consumption variables (*num_mong1*, *num_mong2*, *safe_mong*, *meat_mong*), the null hypothesis that $b_1 = b_2 = b_3 = 0$ was not rejected at the 10 % level, indicating that the flexibility in our RCT had no impact on household-level food consumption behavior during *monga* in 2011. When examining individual parameters, we find that none of them are statistically significant if we use the traditional threshold of the 5 % level. In the equation for *num_mong1* (number of stomach-full meals per day during *monga*), parameter b_2 (the impact of Flexible 1 + IGA) is positive and statistically significant at the 10 % level. The estimated parameter suggests that these borrowers were 14.4 % points more likely to have an additional stomach-full meal. However, when the significance level is set at 20 %, we find that these borrowers were also 14.6 % points less likely to have meat within one of the months of *monga*. One explanation could be the enhanced need for money to undertake IGA activities that do not yield immediate income gains, combined with limited consumption-smoothing abilities. The combination of these factors implies that those borrowers under Flexible 1 + IGA were likely to have spent more on the IGA business at the expense of meat consumption.[7] However, testing of this explanation will be left for future research.

[7] Note that credit was given just before the lean season. As a result, if the borrower wanted to use the credit for business investment, it was more likely that her household would reduce consumption (or, at least, not increase it) and try to divert as much money as possible to the business (Banerjee and Duflo 2011, p. 171). We could then expect that once the business started to earn revenue, the household might increase its consumption.

Table 7.3 Impact of flexible microcredit on food consumption during *Monga* 2011

	Dependent variables			
	num_mong1	*num_mong2*	*safe_mong*	*meat_mong*
Intercept	2.096***	1.708***	0.697***	0.837***
	[0.043]	[0.074]	[0.075]	[0.040]
*D*1 (dummy for flexible 1)	0.009	0.025	0.028	−0.077
	[0.066]	[0.086]	[0.088]	[0.061]
*D*2 (dummy for flexible 1 + IGA)	0.144*	0.012	−0.005	−0.146
	[0.075]	[0.110]	[0.102]	[0.089]
*D*3 (dummy for flexible 2)	−0.020	−0.053	−0.070	−0.093
	[0.056]	[0.092]	[0.088]	[0.057]
*D*4 (dummy for non-borrower)	0.012	−0.036	−0.039	−0.082*
	[0.053]	[0.075]	[0.075]	[0.045]
R^2	0.014	0.004	0.006	0.008
F-stat. for zero slopes of all dummies	1.43	0.52	0.75	1.10
F-stat. for zero slopes of *D*1, *D*2, and *D*3	1.84	0.43	0.81	1.41
Number of observations	1,414	1,412	1,412	1,414

Notes Robust standard errors clustered at the village level are shown in brackets. Significant at the 10 % (*), 5 % (**), and 1 % (***) levels
Source Estimated by the author from the microdata described in the text

Parameter b_4 was estimated with the expected negative sign in three of the four equations, but its absolute value was small; it was also statistically insignificant in all four equations when using the 5 % significance level. In the equation for *meat_mong* (dummy for food security regarding meat consumption), parameter b_4 (the impact of non-borrowers) is negative and statistically significant at the 10 % level. This parameter suggests that microcredit borrowers (regardless of the flexibility type) were 8 % points more likely to have meat in a month (versus the sample average of 76 %). This suggests that microcredit plays a consumption-smoothing role during the lean season. As this parameter is estimated imprecisely overall, the null hypothesis $b_1 = b_2 = b_3 = b_4 = 0$ is not rejected, even at the 20 % level.

Results regarding the impact of our RCT on food consumption during normal, non-*monga* times in 2012 are reported in Table 7.4. When the number of minimum stomach-full meals per day during these normal times (*num_norm2*) was used as the dependent variable, all coefficients on the four dummy variables were small in absolute terms, and the null hypothesis that $b_1 = b_2 = b_3 = b_4 = 0$ was not rejected at the 20 % level. However, when the same variable was transformed as a dummy for food security during normal times (*safe_norm*), the impact of Flexible 2, b_3, was negative, although significant at only the 10 % level. The estimated parameter suggests that such borrowers were 8 % points less likely to be food-secure when compared with the sample average of 89 %. This marks a welfare loss associated with flexible microcredit, which remains a puzzle. When the dependent variable is *safe_norm*, the point estimate for b_4 is −0.069 and statistically significant at the 10 % level. The estimated parameter indicates that non-borrowers

Table 7.4 Impact of flexible microcredit on food consumption during normal times in 2012

	Dependent variables	
	num_norm2	*safe_norm*
Intercept	2.140***	0.933***
	[0.055]	[0.030]
*D*1 (dummy for flexible 1)	−0.042	−0.062
	[0.075]	[0.039]
*D*2 (dummy for flexible 1 + IGA)	0.088	0.033
	[0.080]	[0.033]
*D*3 (dummy for flexible 2)	−0.037	−0.076*
	[0.083]	[0.042]
*D*4 (dummy for non-borrower)	−0.018	−0.069*
	[0.070]	[0.036]
R^2	0.005	0.014
F-stat. for zero slopes of all dummies	0.84	5.38***
F-stat. for zero slopes of *D*1, *D*2, and *D*3	1.12	5.72***

Notes The number of observations is 1,415. Robust standard errors clustered at the village level are shown in brackets. Significant at the 10 % (*), 5 % (**), and 1 % (***) levels
Source Estimated by the author, using the microdata described in the text

were 7 % points more likely to be food-insecure. This evidence weakly supports the favorable impact of credit provision in enhancing consumption.

The results reported in Tables 7.3 and 7.4 were robustly found from other specifications.[8] We tried (i) extending model (7.1) with baseline village and household attributes as additional explanatory variables; (ii) extending the last term in Eq. (7.1), b_4D_{4h}, to have different slopes depending on the treatment arms; (iii) re-estimating Eq. (7.1) without the last term, while using borrower households only; and (iv) using the limited dependent variable models, considering the truncation or integer nature of the dependent variables. The robustness check results from extension (i) are reported in Tables 7.5 and 7.6. Out of the 9 village-level variables analyzed in the balance check in Chap. 5, the distance to the nearest town and the distance to a Hindu temple were included as village-level controls, since these two variables were associated with a marginal failure of the balance check. Similarly, from the 20 household-level variables analyzed in Chap. 5, household size, average age of members, ratio of adults, and the literacy rate of adult females were included as household-level controls, since they were associated with a marginal failure of the balance check (see Tables 5.4, 5.5, 5.6, 5.7). The addition of these 6 controls did not alter the coefficients substantially, nor test results regarding the 4 parameters of interest: b_1, b_2, b_3, and b_4. One small change was that the 3 coefficients that were significant at the 10 % level in Tables 7.3 and 7.4 became significant at the 20 % level only.

[8] The full robustness check results are not reported here, but are available upon request.

Table 7.5 Impact of flexible microcredit on food consumption during *Monga* 2011 (with baseline controls)

	Dependent variables			
	num_mong1	*num_mong2*	*safe_mong*	*meat_mong*
Baseline village characteristics				
Mondir (Hindu temple)	0.078	0.145**	0.144*	0.049
	[0.092]	[0.065]	[0.074]	[0.053]
Town	−0.124	−0.045	−0.046	−0.002
	[0.086]	[0.087]	[0.094]	[0.078]
Baseline household characteristics				
Household size (number of members)	0.031***	0.019	0.020*	0.020**
	[0.012]	[0.012]	[0.011]	[0.009]
Average age of household members	−0.001	0.000	0.000	−0.001
	[0.001]	[0.001]	[0.001]	[0.001]
Ratio of adults (age 15+)	0.230**	−0.016	0.013	0.079
	[0.087]	[0.067]	[0.061]	[0.057]
Literacy rate of adult females	0.093***	0.012	0.013	0.032
	[0.033]	[0.030]	[0.029]	[0.039]
Treatment status				
*D*1 (Dummy for flexible 1)	−0.006	0.028	0.031	−0.074
	[0.068]	[0.093]	[0.095]	[0.063]
*D*2 (Dummy for flexible 1 + IGA)	0.109	0.024	0.006	−0.143
	[0.074]	[0.118]	[0.110]	[0.091]
*D*3 (Dummy for flexible 2)	−0.027	−0.022	−0.037	−0.080
	[0.063]	[0.100]	[0.097]	[0.058]
*D*4 (Dummy for non-borrower)	0.002	−0.017	−0.020	−0.073
	[0.055]	[0.083]	[0.083]	[0.045]
Intercept	1.843***	1.590***	0.552***	0.715***
	[0.109]	[0.127]	[0.125]	[0.085]
R^2	0.040	0.015	0.019	0.014
F-stat. for zero slopes of all explan. variables	2.72***	1.23	1.36	0.92
F-stat. for zero slopes of *D*1, *D*2, *D*3, and *D*4	1.26	0.26	0.36	0.91
F-stat. for zero slopes of *D*1, *D*2, and *D*3	1.66	0.17	0.35	1.18
Number of observations	1,414	1,412	1,412	1,414

Notes Robust standard errors clustered at the village level are shown in brackets. Significant at the 10 % (*), 5 % (**), and 1 % (***) levels

Source Estimated by the author, using the microdata described in the text

Table 7.6 Impact of flexible microcredit on food consumption during normal times in 2012 (with baseline controls)

	Dependent variables	
	num_norm2	*safe_norm*
Baseline village characteristics		
Mondir (Hindu temple)	0.018	0.027
	[0.075]	[0.035]
Town	0.049	0.036
	[0.103]	[0.033]
Baseline household characteristics		
Household size (number of members)	0.058***	0.026***
	[0.013]	[0.007]
Average age of household members	−0.003	0.000
	[0.002]	[0.001]
Ratio of adults (age 15+)	0.222**	0.06
	[0.090]	[0.045]
Literacy rate of adult females	0.001	−0.029
	[0.043]	[0.023]
Treatment status		
*D*1 (dummy for flexible 1)	−0.040	−0.057
	[0.077]	[0.038]
*D*2 (dummy for flexible 1 + IGA)	0.092	0.046
	[0.083]	[0.033]
*D*3 (dummy for flexible 2)	−0.024	−0.060
	[0.087]	[0.042]
*D*4 (dummy for non-borrower)	−0.006	−0.057
	[0.068]	[0.035]
Intercept	1.849***	0.792***
	[0.133]	[0.061]
R^2	0.023	0.030
F-stat. for zero slopes of all explan. variables	2.74***	3.23***
F-stat. for zero slopes of *D*1, *D*2, *D*3, and *D*4	0.82	5.44***
F-stat. for zero slopes of *D*1, *D*2, and *D*3	1.07	6.45***

Notes The number of observations is 1,415. Robust standard errors clustered at the village level are shown in brackets. Significant at the 10 % (*), 5 % (**), and 1 % (***) levels
Source Estimated by the author, using the microdata described in the text

7.5 Conclusion

This chapter empirically assessed whether a flexible repayment design for microcredit could enhance food consumption among the ultra-poor. We used a cross-section dataset collected in northern Bangladesh in 2012 after the implementation of RCT in 2011–2012. We found repayment flexibility to have no positive impact on food consumption during or immediately after the period under the RCT intervention. However, all microcredit borrowers tended to have more secure food consumption than non-borrowers, although the difference was marginal.

The finding of the difficulty in pinpointing a positive impact of microcredit on food consumption is consistent with the literature on microcredit in Bangladesh (e.g., Roodman and Morduch 2009). Our finding that repayment flexibility had no positive impact on consumption may appear inconsistent with the finding of Czura et al. (2011), who found that flexible repayment schedules resulted in smoother consumption, and with the findings of Shoji (2010), who found that rescheduling substantially decreased the probability of meal-skipping among borrowers. However, our finding is not inconsistent with that of Czura et al. (2011) because they also show a lack of difference in consumption *levels* between borrowers under standard and flexible repayment schedules. Neither is it inconsistent with that of Shoji (2010), since his analysis focused on emergency cases involving flooding, when rescheduling would have immediately affected food consumption, whereas our experiment was conducted under normal conditions.

In the context of the current study, we suggest several possible explanations for the insignificant impact of repayment flexibility. First, if the main route through which the provision of microcredit enhances consumption is the reduction of liquidity constraints, our findings are consistent with the view that the main problem for the ultra-poor is consumption smoothing between the *monga* and non-*monga* seasons, as they were already able to smooth consumption within each season even in the absence of microcredit. If this is the case—and both income and price effects are negligible—then there should be no difference across microcredit types, but non-borrowers' consumption should be smaller than that of borrowers. Our empirical results broadly support this pattern. The unexpected negative coefficient of the impact of repayment moratoria with IGA support in the regression for meat consumption during *monga* is consistent with this view as well: borrowers under this scheme experienced difficulty in smoothing resources between the current *monga* period and the future, and they were compelled to spend more on their IGA. Second, the insignificant impact of repayment flexibility could be due to the insignificant difference in income changes across the four credit schemes studied. This was likely when the borrowed money was invested in a business that did not generate immediate income gains. Third, the overall insignificance of regression on food consumption could be due to the treated households' perception of the transient nature of the intervention. If the borrower households perceived the change brought by microcredit—be it an income, price, or liquidity effect—as a one-time phenomenon, they did not realize that their permanent income (in terms of both level and variability) and credit-access positions had improved. If this is the case, rational households may not adjust their consumption.

These interpretations are speculative, however. Analysis of the impact of flexible repayment on household income and consumption over a longer horizon is left for further analysis.

7.6 Appendix

Regarding the attrition, we regressed the dropout dummy on the village and household characteristics. We found these variables had no explanatory power, as shown in Table 7.7.

Table 7.7 Correlates of attrition

	Dependent variable: dummy for attrition
Baseline village characteristics	
Mondir (Hindu temple)	0.0002
	[0.0076]
Town	0.0226
	[0.0185]
Baseline household characteristics	
Household size (number of members)	0.0012
	[0.0018]
Average age of household members	−0.0003
	[0.0003]
Ratio of adults (age 15+)	−0.0141
	[0.0170]
Literacy rate of adult females	0.0160
	[0.0104]
Intercept	0.0224
	[0.0193]
R^2	0.010
F-stat. for zero slopes of all explan. variables	1.72

Notes The number of observations is 1,440. Robust standard errors clustered at the village level are shown in brackets. None of these values are significant at the 10 % level
Source Compiled by the author from baseline survey data

References

Banerjee AV, Duflo E (2011) Poor economics: a radical rethinking of the way to fight global poverty. Public Affairs

Czura K, Karlan D, Mullainathan S (2011) Does flexibility in microfinance pay off? Evidence from a randomized evaluation in rural India. Paper presented at the NEUDC 2011 conference

Roodman D, Morduch J (2009) The impact of microcredit on the poor in Bangladesh: revisiting the evidence. Working paper 174, center for global development

Shoji Masahiro (2010) Does contingent repayment in microfinance help the poor during natural disasters? J Dev Stud 46(2):191–210

Chapter 8
Concluding Remarks

Abu S. Shonchoy

Abstract We combined a cross-sectional survey dataset with a randomized control trial (RCT) experiment to test the impact of relaxing typical microcredit payment rules with regard to each of the following: food consumption, loan repayments, and loan default behavior. Our analysis suggest no systematic difference among the treatment arms in case of default, overdue amount, or repayment frequency. On the other hand, we find no positive impact of the repayment flexibility on immediate food consumption during the period of seasonality.

Keywords Microcredit · Default · Seasonality · Consumption smoothing · Bangladesh

The emergence of microcredit institutions has been a recent policy development in poverty alleviation in developing countries. These institutions have given the poor improved access to the formal credit market. However, the interactions and side effects of this policy instrument have not yet been studied extensively, despite their being of tremendous importance in any evaluation of it. Based on anecdotal and survey-based evidence, we find that strict microcredit schemes can actually lower the welfare of rural people during times of seasonal hardship and temporary unemployment. To the best of our knowledge, this problem has not been adequately studied within the literature, even though it has direct implications vis-à-vis development policy. This research gap points to the need, importance, and relevance of a comprehensive and methodologically sound study of the problem—a gap that this study looks to fill, at least in part.

In an attempt to enhance the welfare level of the ultra-poor, this study aims to understand the impact of flexible microcredit repayment on the poor, seasonality-affected, and vulnerable people of northern Bangladesh. We combined a cross-sectional survey dataset with a randomized control trial (RCT) experiment to test

A. S. Shonchoy (✉)
Institute of Developing Economies, Japan External Trade Organization,
3-2-2 Wakaba, Mihama-ku, Chiba-shi 261-8545, Japan
e-mail: parves.shonchoy@gmail.com

A. S. Shonchoy (ed.), *Seasonality and Microcredit*, SpringerBriefs in Economics,
DOI: 10.1007/978-4-431-55010-5_8,

the impact of relaxing these payment rules with regard to each of the following: food consumption, loan repayments, and loan default behavior.

One of the primary aims of this project was to rigorously understand the frequency of loan repayments and the delinquency of borrowers to which various treatment interventions had been applied. The results of our descriptive analysis suggest that the seasonal factors that several borrowers in various locations face bring about similar patterns of repayment behavior. Nonetheless, the vulnerability, seasonality, and adversity faced by *char* dwellers are of an extreme nature, and this is reflected in their repayment patterns. On the other hand, the results of our descriptive analysis of various microcredit products suggest that the provision of illiquid microcredit (where an asset is provided, instead of liquid credit) may not be able to create immediate income, as we found there to be slight patterns of rising default and delinquency levels, within the "Flexible 1 + IGA" treatment arm, compared to those of the other loan products. It might suggest the asset that they had chosen may not have generated immediate enough revenue to allow regular payments, and, as a result, they suffered the consequences of moderately higher default rates and delinquency levels.

Based on a short *monga* survey—which gave rise to a dataset collected in 2011, immediately following the RCT implementation—we empirically assessed the impact of seasonality-adjusted flexible microcredit on food consumption and loan repayments among borrowing households. We found repayment flexibility to have no positive impact on food consumption. On the other hand, all microcredit borrowers tended to have more secure food consumption than non-borrowers, although the difference was marginal. Our finding of the non-significant impact of microcredit on food consumption is consistent with the literature on microcredit in Bangladesh (e.g., Roodman and Morduch 2013). This finding could be due to the possibility that treated households perceive the transient nature of the intervention, or perceive that the main form of liquidity constraint in the study area was resource allocation between seasons, rather than within a season. An alternative explanation for this finding is that borrowed money is sometimes invested in businesses that do not generate immediate income gains, or that the borrower wanted to save the credit for a business investment, rather than to increase consumption. Another alternative explanation could be that households in the region of the study were already used to with a reduce food habit during the lean season as their traditional coping strategy, which they did not want to chance even with the flexible microcredit repayment structure. These interpretations are nonetheless tentative, and an analysis of the impact of a flexible repayment system on household income and consumption requires longer-horizon data.

In the empirical analysis of loan repayments, we gathered information vis-à-vis the general opinions of MFIs in Bangladesh for not offering seasonality-adjusted microcredit products. They stated two reasons for not providing any flexibility or seasonal adjustments during the period of *monga*: (1) it might break the borrowers' loan repayment discipline, and (2) it might increase the rate of loan defaults. Using an RCT field experiment in northern Bangladesh, we randomly assigned seasonality-adjusted flexible microcredit and traditional rigid microcredit schemes to various borrowing groups. Our results suggest that there were no statistically discernible differences among the treatment arms in terms of defaults or overdue amounts, so the findings support the provision of flexible microcredit repayment terms. Even after allowing the loan collection discipline some flexibility and a moratorium (50 %, if the borrowers were under a full moratorium during *monga*), the nongovernment organization with which we partnered managed a recovery rate of more than 95 % of its targeted amount of credit with interest, so its microcredit model can be considered a successful one.

The findings of this study will help MFIs optimize their credit schemes. They could also help other interested parties, including governmental institutions, advocate a relaxation of microcredit rules, or search for alternative policy instruments.

We encountered various issues while writing this book, and they need to be addressed in future research. For example, many of the coefficients had the expected signs, but they were not statistically significant. Adding greater variation through the implementation of additional rounds of surveys could enhance the precision of the estimations. We also need to investigate more carefully whether the findings observed herein are robust, by adding more controls and geographical interaction. This would have increased the statistical power of our estimations. Additionally, to observe behavioral changes in terms of food consumption and with respect to other household decisions, we need to make use of a dataset featuring a longer time horizon.

Reference

Roodman D, Morduch J (2013) The impact of microcredit on the poor in Bangladesh: revisiting the evidence. J Dev Stud (ahead-of-print)

MIX
Papier aus verantwortungsvollen Quellen
Paper from responsible sources
FSC® C105338

If you have any concerns about our products,
you can contact us on
ProductSafety@springernature.com

In case Publisher is established outside the EU,
the EU authorized representative is:
Springer Nature Customer Service Center GmbH
Europaplatz 3, 69115 Heidelberg, Germany

Printed by Libri Plureos GmbH
in Hamburg, Germany